Europe and America:
A Return to History

Europe and America: A Return to History

Miles Kahler

and

Werner Link

COUNCIL ON FOREIGN RELATIONS PRESS

NEW YORK

The Council on Foreign Relations, Inc., is a nonprofit and nonpartisan organization devoted to promoting improved understanding of international affairs through the free exchange of ideas. The Council does not take any position on questions of foreign policy and has no affiliation with, and receives no funding from, the United States government.

If you would like more information on Council publications, please write the Council on Foreign Relations, 58 East 68th Street, New York, NY 10021, or call the Publications Office at (212)734-0400.

Printed in the United States of America.

Library of Congress Cataloging-in-Publication Data

Kahler, Miles, 1949–
Europe and America : a return to history / Miles Kahler and Werner Link.
p. cm.
Includes bibliographical references and index.
ISBN 0-87609-184-2
1. Europe—Foreign relations—United States. 2. United States—Foreign relations—Europe. I. Link, Werner. II. Title.
D34.U5K34 1996
327.4073909904—dc20 95-45164
CIP

96 97 98 PB 10 9 8 7 6 5 4 3 2 1

Cover Design: Dorothy Wachtenheim

Contents

Foreword

Americans continue to feel a special affinity for Europe. So too do Europeans consider their relationship with North American to be unique. These distinct, if ambiguous, shared sentiments undergird the transatlantic community.

But what is the foundation for these sentiments? Are they but legacies of the Cold War and remnants of attitudes forged when Americans and Europeans banded together to resist Soviet communism? Or do they have a more enduring foundation—one that will ensure the existence and vitality of the transatlantic community even in the absence of a dominant external threat? The two essays in this book reflect on these central questions. Taken together, they probe the transatlantic past as well as our understanding of it, seeking to draw lessons and guidance for the future.

Miles Kahler begins by questioning the prevailing narrative of transatlantic relations. He casts doubt on the widely accepted notion that the strength and durability of U.S.-European ties have been the product primarily of external threat. This view represents a myth, Kahler argues, one now being employed instrumentally by those calling for American retrenchment and even retreat from Europe.

By examining periods prior to the onset of the Cold War, Kahler underscores that the transatlantic community has deep economic and cultural roots. During the interwar years, the United States did not engage in feckless isolationism. The decade before the Depression was one of deep American engagement in European economic affairs. A fresh reading of the transatlantic past also points to strong cultural and ideological affinities between the United States and Europe.

Kahler admonishes that constructing this new narrative does not necessarily mean that the United States and Europe will continue to enjoy a partnership as cooperative and close as that of the Cold War. As Europe seeks to unify and as domestic political demands on both sides of the Atlantic mount, the relationship could experience new frictions or at least enter a period of drift. Nonetheless, it is important to discard old paradigms lest they lead us to conclusions too mired in the past—and a misunderstood past at that.

Werner Link takes a different, but equally fresh, tack. He examines chronologically the blueprints that have informed U.S.-European relations over the past century. By thinking through how geopolitics and politics have interacted to produce many different versions of a recurring puzzle, Link offers a useful catalogue of competing paradigms for thinking about the future. His essay offers not just perspective for recasting the transatlantic community, but also a masterful interpretation and synthesis of the past.

Whereas Kahler wants to debunk a misleading narrative, Link argues that different narratives compete during different historical periods. Both agree, however, that external threat is only one color in a complex collage, and that the end of the Cold War by no means foreordains the erosion of the transatlantic community.

This book is sure to become a staple for those who study historical analogies as well as for those concerned about the future of the transatlantic relationship. We are indebted to Miles Kahler and Werner Link for their significant contributions.

Leslie H. Gelb
President of the Council
on Foreign Relations,
New York

Werner Wiedenfeld
Member of the Board of
the Bertelsmann Foundation;
Director of the Research Group
on European Affairs,
University of Munich

Revision and Prevision: Historical Interpretation and the Future of the Transatlantic Relationship

Miles Kahler

1. INTRODUCTION

The use and abuse of history has not received as much attention in the making of America's European policy (or Europe's American policies) as it has in other, more controversial areas, such as American intervention in the Third World or the West's Cold War stance toward the Soviet Union. Perhaps that lack of concern signifies an accurate reading of the historical record in American relations with Europe. Another possibility—and one that I will argue here—is that the Atlantic consensus was sustained by a set of "useful myths" about transatlantic relations before the Cold War that were so powerful and so monolithic that alternative readings of history were virtually excluded from public discourse. This compendium I will label the "internationalist narrative." In using the word "myth," I do not mean to imply that these particular views of transatlantic history are false. In fact, they represent one respected and partially accurate strand of historical opinion regarding American foreign policy in this century. That narrative, however, has received critical scrutiny from historians, despite its resilience among both foreign-policy makers and the wider public. Today, paradoxically, the internationalist myth is as useful for those critical of its liberal and internationalist implications as it once was for advocates of Cold War engagement in Europe.

In a sense, this argument about the gap between historical accounts of transatlantic relations in this century and the dominant myth about them concerns the sources of those historical analogies, whose use and misuse by policymakers has been so ably documented by Ernest May, Richard Neustadt, and Yuen Foong Khong.[1] Some of the most powerful historical analogies employed by policymakers are drawn directly from personal recollection and experience, but others derive at least part of their power from a wider resonance in foreign policy publics and the electorate.

As May makes clear, the connection between these conceptions of the past and the work of professional historians is often tenuous. Historians may participate in the construction of such favored and pervasive narratives, but often the sources of these analogies lie in the common experience of political generations, the simplified history presented in school texts, or the "lessons" declaimed by politicians. Quite apart from such cognitive sources, these analogies may also be part of powerful ideologies attached to particular social or bureaucratic interests. They may legitimate a claim on resources or undergird particular policies.

Once constructed, these images of the past may take on an independent life that traces a path distant from the trajectory of historical research. The testing and questioning of these dominant interpretations is made more difficult by the fact that historians themselves are influenced by compelling political conflicts of their times; historical truth is seldom consensual and uncontested. A more tentative and questioning view of historical "facts" might also be prevented by the fact that bad history may support useful social ends and become connected to apparently successful international outcomes. Using bad history in the pursuit of disastrous outcomes is clearly a major source of concern over the abuses of history by policymakers and publics; bad history that produces good ends is rarely the object of dissection or anxiety.[2]

In juxtaposing the internationalist narrative of transatlantic relations with alternatives drawn from recent historical research, two of the strategies suggested by May and Neustadt will prove useful. One is conceiving history as a stream: pushing back the examination of Europe's relations with the United States beyond the great rupture of World War II and the Cold War, which serves as a starting point for a completely new chapter in the conventional account. Benchmarks are important in history; the apparently new world of the Cold War and the Atlantic alliance may appear in a different light when historical comparison is pushed further into the past. The other strategy that May and Neustadt described is the construction of categories of likeness and difference, an exercise that calls into question any simple prediction of "back to the future." Such an exercise forgoes the simplicity of a dominant analogy for the complexity of a model built on several dimensions. Carefully tracing differences and similarities between post–Cold War and pre–Cold War eras suggests that both internationalist fears and isolationist nostalgia are misplaced. First, however, the internationalist narrative must be delineated, and its transformation, from bulwark of internationalism to instrument of its critics, explored.

2. TRANSATLANTIC HISTORY AND THE POST–COLD WAR FOREIGN POLICY DEBATE

In the internationalist account that has dominated our view of transatlantic relations in this century, *threat* is the dynamic of American relations with Europe, and *rupture* is the dominant pattern. The United States, in this view, yearned for separation from the European balance of power—a corrupting game that did not affect American interests. Nevertheless, the European war that began in 1914 and the attacks on neutral rights that it spawned eventually engulfed the United States. Despite the efforts of President Woodrow Wilson and his supporters to cement American engagement in Europe, the defeat of the Treaty of Versailles marked the beginning of two decades of isolationism, during which the United States mistakenly believed that it could retreat to its historical policy of distancing itself from European conflicts. At the same time, economic nationalism supported a shortsighted policy of American unilateralism and protectionism in economic policy that deepened and lengthened the Great Depression. Only a renewed threat of Hitler's Germany and the Japanese attack on Pearl Harbor was able, very belatedly, to erode American unwillingness to involve itself directly in ensuring a balance of power in Europe. The Soviet threat during the Cold War produced at long last a widespread consensus in the United States that the security and prosperity of Western Europe was a vital American interest, one ensured by the North Atlantic Treaty, a security guarantee made credible by the stationing of American troops in Europe. In addition, the Cold War alliance had an economic corollary: clear support should be given for a multilateral trading and financial order committed to liberal principles, even though America's economic partners often pursued less than liberal policies.

This simplified history of the transatlantic relationship has played an important and nearly unquestioned part in the U.S. commitment to Europe and in European acceptance of that engagement. Transatlantic history before 1945 is a seamless story of isolationism broken only by the brief intervention of 1917–19. World War II and the Cold War are then portrayed as grim learning experiences that permitted the United States to banish the shortsighted isolationism and protectionism of earlier decades in this century. Note as well that this is an *American* narrative, whether recounted in Europe or the United States: changes in American policy define the transatlantic relationship, an assumption of dependency that seemed to fit with the pattern of the Cold War alliance. The internationalist history of transatlantic relations also awards primacy to military and political features of international politics, rather than economic or cultural ones. It reflects the synthesis between realism and internationalism forged during the Truman and Eisenhower administrations, a synthesis that remained untroubled until the Vietnam War. Internationalism in this case is liberal internationalism in its economic prescriptions, but not in its assessment of the dynamics of world politics.

Despite the political usefulness of this historical narrative, proponents of transatlantic cooperation and existing alliance structures have discovered that the internationalist account has been stood on its head by critics of the internationalist consensus. The dominant myth attached transatlantic cooperation to what seemed a secure anchor: a common external threat. Since the Soviet threat was unlikely to disappear, the foundations of the relationship appeared to be deeply embedded in the international order. Now, with the end of the Cold War and the removal of the Russian military threat from Central Europe, this useful myth has, ironically, been taken up by those arguing for American retrenchment and economic nationalism.

Realist critiques of existing transatlantic structures take several forms. One is a simple empirical argument based on neorealist theory: since alliances emerge to meet perceived threats, the disappearance of the Soviet threat means that the NATO alliance will eventually disappear.[3] John Mearsheimer has advanced more radical predictions, arguing that the end of bipolarity and the emergence of a multipolar system in Europe will inevitably produce balancing behavior similar to that of great power systems in the past.[4] More germane to immediate American policies toward Europe are suggestions that the Cold War pattern of transatlantic relations was an aberration and that the United States can now return to a more "natural" past of disengagement from its security and economic responsibilities in Europe. Even James Schlesinger, a confirmed Atlanticist, has asked what is "to succeed the security arrangements in providing the glue that maintains American involvement in Europe," and argued (joining a virtually unanimous chorus) that the United States must focus on its domestic problems.[5]

Although Schlesinger argues for a renewed and reshaped partnership, other realist isolationists endorse more radical changes. In an assault on what they see as a persistent strategy of American preponderance, Christopher Layne and Benjamin Schwartz argue that the United States would have pursued a policy of global imperial overstretch during the Cold War in the absence of the Soviet threat. The Soviet "foil" was essential, however, in selling that strategy to both the American public and European allies. With the demise of this "convenient adversary," realism and internationalism, in uneasy balance since 1945, can now be unraveled. Although their positive program remains unclear, the rhetoric of Layne and Schwartz is neo-isolationist: the United States confronts an unchanging world politics of "war, instability, great power security and economic rivalries, multipolarity, and the formation of power balances," yet it lives "in a safe neighborhood," enjoying "relative immunity from external threat."[6] In similar fashion, Owen Harries contends that the notion of "the West" is entirely a function of military threat. With the dissolution of the Soviet Union, "the odds are somewhat against" a persistence of "close American association with Europe in that enterprise."[7] In these accounts, the tug of domestic needs combines with the demise of the Soviet threat to produce a sweeping transformation of transatlantic relations. The new realist tack shares with the old internationalist narrative a vision of a pre–Cold War America that was utterly remote from the balances in Europe and East Asia, but these arguments deviate from the internationalist account in viewing that state of affairs with nostalgia. Perhaps the United States should retire once again to its "safe neighborhood," now that the imminent threats of the past half century have disappeared.

The end of the Cold War has also provided an opportunity for calling into question the resilience of economic internationalism. In this view, the Cold War was not only a guarantee of American involvement in Europe but also an irreplaceable glue to sustain Western economic cooperation. The passing of the Soviet threat will mean renewed economic nationalism and international conflict, and quite possibly the disintegration of existing, enfeebled multilateral economic institutions. For Lester Thurow, the image of economic warfare among three blocs (predicted by neorealists since the early 1970s) is dominant.[8] Jeffrey Garten argues that "we have to accept that the Cold War was a unique period, and that the changes that will now occur will go well beyond what America has been willing to concede."[9] A group of scholars at Berkeley express pessimism that existing global institutions can manage the new economic conflicts that will emerge "now that a common and dominant Soviet enemy no longer exists."[10]

For these critics of an internationalist and multilateral image of the future, the Cold War established a particular security and economic order, which is now bound to disappear. The relations between the United States and Europe will now return to a more "natural" conflictual state in a multipolar international system. Oddly, the "natural" state of affairs before the grand divide of World War II and the Cold War is never described; the implicit image of those decades mirrors the internationalist narrative: a United States disengaged from Western Europe, pursuing its limited national interests in a secure hemispheric cocoon, espousing economic nationalism and eschewing cooperative ventures with its rivals across the Atlantic. Since the decades before 1940 are such a crucial benchmark for these predictions about the post–Cold War world, it is worth reexamining that history more closely to see if this peculiar image of past transatlantic relations—Arcadia for realist isolationists, anathema for liberal internationalists—did in fact exist.

3. EUROPE AND THE UNITED STATES IN THE ERA OF IMPERIALISM

The decades antedating the first American military intervention in Europe are now so distant that their usefulness for charting contemporary transatlantic ties may appear insignificant. Nevertheless, the period before 1917 is important in tracing two patterns that emerged early on and persisted throughout the century. First, for as long as the United States has been a major industrial power, it has impinged upon Europe (and been impinged upon by the European powers) *outside* Europe. Second, American relations with Europe were not characterized, even in that more remote period, by equidistant balancing among the European powers.

As the United States underwent its extraordinarily rapid industrialization during the late nineteenth century, its international presence ceased to be peripheral to the European powers. What would now be labeled "out-of-area" conflicts increased in frequency and intensity: the United States might remain distant from European balancing, but Europe did not always remain distant from American traders, investors, and missionaries. American industrialization extended the range of U.S. interests from its immediate neighbors (in particular Canada, which had long served as a lever against Britain) to the Caribbean, Latin America, and the Pacific.

Conflict between the United States and the European powers over their respective imperial ambitions would last into the era of NATO and decolonization, when the most bitter conflicts between the United States and its allies often arose over policies toward peripheral areas. In this earliest era of extra-European conflict, a mirror image of the pattern of imperialist competition also emerged: growing anxiety on the part of the United States over European intrusions into the Western Hemisphere. If European statesmen saw an industrializing and expansive newcomer as a threat to their established imperial positions, the United States still feared European encroachment in its hemispheric "backyard." The hostility of the American elite and public toward Britain for much of the nineteenth century (and toward France during its brief Mexican adventure) was driven in large measure by perceived threats to the Western Hemisphere. Early cordiality toward Prussia/Germany was shaped by perceptions that Germany had no such ambitions.

After 1890, however, Germany's *Weltpolitik*, its economic penetration of Latin America, and its rivalries with the United States over insignificant but politically sensitive outposts such as Samoa created a growing perception in the United States of hostile German ambitions. Throughout the twentieth century, a United States that isolationists claimed could retreat to its hemisphere was in a state of almost perpetual alarm over the security of its particular sphere of influence, and the threats that it perceived in that quarter—whether perceived accurately or not—were often transferred to broader definitions of hostile intentions. The United States undertook the Spanish-American War in part because of fears that continuing conflict in Cuba would embroil the European powers; suspicions of Wilhelmine Germany were transformed into hostility by the Zimmermann telegram, which broached a hostile alliance with

Mexico; Nazi subversion in South America absorbed the Roosevelt administration.[11] (And, of course, American hypersensitivity persisted into the Cold War, from Guatemala to Cuba to the Central American interventions of the Reagan administration.)

Since the eruption of the United States as a competitor with the European powers around the globe "appeared to many observers to be nothing less than revolutionary," it was hardly surprising that grating conflicts would occur as Europe accustomed itself to the newcomer.[12] What was striking, however, was the speed with which the United States aligned itself with one European power, Britain—its former colonial master and an object of political suspicion for much of the nineteenth century—and against another, Germany—a power with which the United States had long enjoyed friendly relations. This rapprochement between what would be the greatest industrial power and the first industrial nation was "not only an astonishing [development], it was also one of the most important in world history of the past hundred years."[13] Although a series of post hoc realist arguments can be constructed to make the Anglo-American alignment appear inevitable, it hardly seemed likely in the early 1890s. Following an earlier historical pattern, some Europeans expected the United States to align itself with one or more continental powers against Britain.[14] American efforts to harden and expand the Monroe Doctrine brought sharp retorts from even the most sympathetic politicians in Britain. Even after the relatively amicable solution to the 1895 Venezuelan crisis, some British observers predicted that the foremost naval power would eventually have to fight first Germany and then the United States.[15] Yet by the turn of the century, American naval planners were gaming a general war in which the Anglo-Saxon powers were part of one coalition and Germany belonged to another.[16]

The question of why the United States tilted toward Britain and not Germany has understandably produced considerable scholarly controversy. Without wading too deeply into those debates, two compelling arguments for the Anglo-American alignment also presage familiar and persistent patterns in later American engagement with Europe. Although characteristics of Britain and Germany have been offered as explanations for American perceptions of threat before 1917—Germany as another rising industrial and naval power might well appear more alarming in American eyes—it was British behavior toward the United States that was far more important. The European powers were not simply sources of threat observed by the American elite and public; they were—and remained throughout the twentieth century—*active* in their approaches to the New World power. After 1895 Britain embarked on a calculated policy of appeasement toward the United States, beginning with its concessions in the 1895 Venezuela crisis, continuing in the negotiation of the Olney-Pauncefote Arbitration Treaty (a remarkable step, even if later overturned by the U.S. Senate), and, above all, clear British signals of understanding and friendship during the Spanish-American War.[17] Britain's concessions were a mirror image of the policy of bluster and pinpricks Germany followed from Samoa to Manila Bay; effusive efforts by Kaiser Wilhelm II to court U.S. President Theodore Roosevelt could not dislodge the earlier distrust. German *Weltpolitik* and naval policy became for the United States, as it had for Britain, a symbol of Germany's broader intentions; Britain's one-sided conciliation, on the other hand, served to overcome British liabilities in American domestic politics.

By the early twentieth century, however, Wilhelmine Germany had more than erratic and provocative foreign policy maneuvers to overcome. A second feature served as an attractive force between Britain and the United States, and an equal source of repulsion between Germany and America: Britain moved in these decades to democratize its liberal political system; the United States perceived Germany, in contrast, as a militarized and dangerous autocracy. The United States, despite its rapid industrialization and naval ambitions, came to support global stability as defined by Britain, and its interests were interpreted as aligned with those of Britain. That interpretation, in a global order broadly defined as liberal, was in large measure a reflection of domestic political systems and ideologies that also converged. Paul Kennedy assigns this perception of a shared political culture equal or greater weight with economic complementarity and British concessions in explaining the Anglo-American alignment.[18] After repeated German efforts to woo the United States, even the convinced imperialist Theodore Roosevelt could not dismiss the importance of its political regime: "the German people are too completely under his [Wilhelm II] rule for me to be able to disassociate them from him. . . . I should never dream of counting on his friendship for this country."[19] On the German side (and in contrast to Britain), agrarian interests, threatened by American exports, launched a broad attack on the influence of the United States in Europe, and particularly its role in spreading democratic principles.[20] Even at this relatively early stage of deepening relations between the United States and Europe, a strong ideological element had appeared. Later in the century, when American isolationism was at its peak, Walter Lippmann pointed out that the policy of political nonentanglement in Europe depended on a world order guaranteed by sea power "controlled by men who on the whole believe in the supremacy of law and in government by consent of the governed."[21] America's engagement in Europe and its definition of the threats emanating from Europe would continue to be shaped strongly by its liberal democratic ideology.

4. THE INTERWAR DECADES AND THE LIMITS OF ISOLATIONISM

Even before 1917, the United States could be defined as a world power. As such, its foreign policy forced it to contend with the European powers.[22] These early interactions exhibited patterns that would persist: an American concern for hemispheric security, conflicting ambitions in non-European parts of the globe, European strategies to shape American opinion and policy, and finally the growing importance of liberal ideology in defining threats and prospective partners in Europe. All of these features of the pre-1914 world suggest that the first rupture in transatlantic relations—World War I—may have been less a great divide than the internationalist narrative portrays. The interwar decades are far more significant in that narrative, however, since they are portrayed as a time of feckless forswearing of global and European responsibilities by the United States, the last "normal" decades before Hitler and Stalin forced an active world role on the United States and confirmed American partnership with the European democracies. Recent historical research, however, has profoundly undermined the Wilsonian narrative of the 1920s and 1930s.

The shift in historical interpretation has been so fundamental that a recent conference of German and American scholars "made it quite clear that no one was prepared to defend the thesis that the United States policy toward Europe could still be interpreted as isolationism."[23] A first generation of historical research that endorsed the (disenchanted) internationalist view of the 1920s and 1930s was transformed first by a wave of revisionism that emphasized the continuity in American economic aims in Europe throughout the period, and then by a wave that emphasized the limits placed by European powers, particularly Britain, on the exercise of American economic and political influence.[24]

The new historical consensus has not overturned the central strategic fact of these decades—that the United States eschewed any formal military commitment to the European order after 1919—but it has qualified the importance of that fact by unearthing a rich story of deep U.S. involvement in the reconstruction of Europe during the 1920s. American policies were broadly shared by both Republicans (typically labeled as the more isolationist and nationalist of the political parties) and Democrats. The American stance could be characterized as "involvement without commitment," an effort to square political demands to remain strategically uncommitted with the promotion of European stability (and American prosperity) through economic engagement.[25]

The motivation for American engagement with European economic recovery remains contested. Revisionists emphasize the economic self-interest revealed by figures such as Charles Evans Hughes, who declared that "we cannot dispose of these problems by calling them European, for they are world problems and we cannot escape the injurious consequences of a failure to settle them. . . . There will be no permanent peace unless economic satisfactions are enjoyed."[26] Whether the American economy was dependent on European markets or not, beliefs in such dependence were widely shared. The United States remained a continental and closed economy by world standards. By the mid-1920s, however, more than seven percent of national industrial production was sold abroad, and the depressed agricultural sector was even more dependent on exports to Europe.[27] Those skeptical of the revisionist emphasis on economic motivations argue that American policymakers "did not generally consider the health of the American economy and polity to depend in the first instance on European recovery."[28]

Whatever the assessment of American motivations, little dispute remains regarding the level of American economic engagement or the instruments of American activism and its goals. Economic nationalism in the 1920s was more tempered than the internationalist account allows. Even such symbols as the Fordney-McCumber Tariff, unquestionably more protectionist than the Underwood Tariff, which preceded it, instituted unconditional most-favored-nation treatment, running counter to the discrimination of the colonial powers.[29] Given the political barriers to formal government "entanglement" in Europe, however, American administrations of the 1920s privatized their European foreign policy. Instead of participating in the reparations commission, the United States preferred to use "independent" committees of financial experts with excellent back-channel communications to Washington. Since New York was the only source for loans on the scale required to make the complicated system of reparations and war debt repayment work, the Federal Reserve Bank of New York and private American bankers, particularly the House of Morgan, exercised enormous power.[30] And since no loan could be floated successfully on the New York market without at least the tacit approval of the U.S. government, the "loose alliance" of "government officials, central bankers, and top private businessmen" who ran America's European initiatives exerted considerable leverage in Europe.[31] The American agenda included "three interlocking components in building a secure world open to trade, investment, and peaceful change": the Dawes Plan, which temporarily transformed the bitter political issue of reparations into a matter of business contracts; war debt settlement; and a return to the gold standard.[32] American endorsement of moderate revisions in the Versailles system was confirmed by the use of American financial leverage to support the Locarno Peace Pact and German membership in the League of Nations.[33] By the end of the decade, American ambitions in Europe had expanded to include disarmament, trade relations organized according to the unconditional most-favored-nation principle, a final settlement of reparations, and European currency stability. The chosen instrument of American policy—economic diplomacy—remained the same.[34]

The degree of competition and cooperation in U.S. economic relations with European powers varied from one policy area to another. The key relationship was with Britain, given its strategic and economic importance. By the mid-1920s, an effective entente had been forged with Britain on issues of international finance, communications (radio and cable), and petroleum in the Middle East. In resource policy, cooperation based on delegation to private corporations and minimal government guidance was harder to achieve.[35] There was also evidence of what would be labeled "system friction" decades later, since the United States favored a larger role for business, and European governments often used government monopolies as their representatives.[36] Nevertheless, the political constraints placed on the American government by congressional and public sentiment did not prevent government-business cooperation in furthering transatlantic diplomatic ends. The form that this strategy took, and particularly the large role awarded to private business, differed dramatically from the intergovernmental institutions that defined post-1945 cooperation. American policy in the 1920s represented internationalism, but it was internationalism of a different kind.

This image of public guidance, private instruments of collaboration, and a relatively high level of collaboration between the United States and Britain on European affairs has been challenged more recently by the so-called London school of historians. They resurrect realist criteria of measuring international influence and reject an economic determinism that has awarded the United States international preeminence after World War II. The conflictual and competitive strand in U.S.-European relations is reasserted, and American policy in Europe is viewed (as it was by earlier realists) as ineffectual and inconsistent.[37] Even this reinjection of self-interest and traditional power politics calculations, however, does not return American policy to its previous isolationist characterization.

This intricate structure for preserving American influence in Europe was based on American private lending and European prosperity. It quickly unraveled with the onset of the Great Depression. The internationalist narrative and its latter-day corollaries allege that the Great Depression worsened because of a failure in international leadership. Britain was incapable of providing for hegemonic stabilization of the world economy, and the United States was unwilling to do so.[38] Historians have viewed the possibility of an American stabilization of the world economy after 1929 with considerable skepticism. Not only did political constraints in the United States prevent public initiatives of a more comprehensive sort, European elites would probably have resisted the "massive intervention" required.[39]

An absence of American leadership may not have been so central in causing the Great Depression to deepen and spread in any case. The major framework for international economic cooperation in the 1920s—the gold standard—had been undermined by World War I and by the democratization of politics in Europe and the United States. As Barry Eichengreen asserts, the gold standard "itself was the principal threat to financial stability and economic prosperity between the wars."[40] The weaknesses of the gold standard were not principally the absence of a dominant financial power, as Charles Kindleberger has argued. The Bank of England may have been the "conductor" of the system before 1914, but even then management was in crucial aspects multipolar. Instead of hegemony, Eichengreen contends that the gold standard weakened because the commitment of governments to the international monetary system was no longer credible in an era of democratic politics and demands for economic stabilization. In addition, the major financial powers were unwilling to create new institutions to sustain cooperation and permit the coordination of reflationary policies when the Depression began. At the same time, many national elites were initially unwilling to let go of the gold standard rules or to entertain policy options other than the deflationary ones instituted by U.S. President Herbert Hoover, German Chancellor Heinrich Brüning, and British Chancellor of the Exchequer Philip Snowden. Their resistance was not simply ideological obstinance; attachment to gold was driven by "rational fears" that abandoning the system would lead to inflation, a "lesson" learned too well in the preceding decade.[41] The central banks of the United States and Europe led their governments into deeper and deeper economic distress until the governments, unable to bear the political costs any longer (or replaced by others who were unwilling to do so), threw off their "golden fetters" and undertook reflation.[42]

This revised view of the international onset of the Great Depression directs attention away from the United States and the final failure of its economic diplomacy in Europe, and toward other sources of economic breakdown: the politicization of economic policy and the weakness of international institutions and the cooperation that they instilled. The Bank for International Settlements, established as part of the Young Plan, could have been a force for cooperative solutions during the Depression, but central bankers and politicians remained too reluctant to part with any portion of their policy autonomy. As the tug of domestic demands became greater, what remained of international cooperation disintegrated, and both the United States and the European powers embarked on a course of economic nationalism and disengagement.

The Depression years unquestionably marked the apogee of estrangement between the United States and Europe, and the peak of American isolationism. Even during those years, however, policy continuities could be observed. Legendary symbols of national shortsightedness such as the Smoot-Hawley Tariff of 1930 were "not prompted by a parochial nationalism that denied the importance of European stability to

American self-interest."[43] Although President Franklin Roosevelt in his early statements held out Wilsonian hopes to the Europeans, the economic nationalists in his inner circle triumphed in the early months of the administration, particularly in his notorious message to the World Economic Conference. The nationalist moment soon passed, however. The United States enacted the Reciprocal Trade Agreements Act, authorizing the president to negotiate tariff reductions, and moved in 1936 toward monetary cooperation with France and Britain through the Tripartite Agreement. Although efforts at multilateral institution-building would not begin in earnest until World War II, the impulse toward economic collaboration had emerged well before the shocks of world war and cold war. A postwar economic order founded on transatlantic cooperation had its origins in disenchantment with the beggar-thy-neighbor nationalism of the 1930s, not in collaboration induced by a common threat to national security.

Roosevelt was even more politically constrained in his European policies than the Republicans had been, given his commitment to an extensive program of domestic reform and his need for isolationist support to enact that program. Nevertheless, familiar patterns in transatlantic relations had resurfaced by the late 1930s, pulling the United States toward closer engagement with the European democracies. Although the internationalist account portrays Europe in the 1920s and 1930s as waiting for a reluctant United States, European attitudes toward American exertions were often ambivalent. Economic rivalries with Britain were compounded by British resentment of American intrusions in the 1920s and by doubts about American reliability in the 1930s.[44] American involvement was often seen as creating more problems than it solved. These reservations diminished in the late 1930s, but they did not fully disappear until the advent of Winston Churchill's government in 1940.

Roosevelt also shared the anxieties of his predecessors regarding European intrusions and subversion in the hemisphere; he increased the American diplomatic presence in the region and deployed hemispheric initiatives like the Good Neighbor Policy to thwart Nazi penetration in Latin America. (The House Un-American Activities Committee began its career ferreting out Nazi subversion in the United States.) Roosevelt and his American supporters also displayed a familiar bias toward support for the European democracies in the 1930s. Although the Democratic administration continued a policy of appeasement toward Fascist Italy, it increasingly defined "threat" and "stability" in Europe in terms of particular non-democratic regimes. In the last years of the decade, ideological themes "quickly assumed astonishing proportions," especially after the Nazi persecution of the Jews became more overt and violent. The United States registered a particularly strong protest after the *Kristallnacht* pogrom of November 9, 1938, and downgraded its diplomatic relations with Germany.[45]

A final dimension of transatlantic relations assumed particular prominence in the interwar decades: cultural exports from the United States to Europe. Before World War I the United States had remained a net cultural borrower from Europe. Language and culture had served to support the gradual alignment of the United States with Britain; strong cultural ties to Germany had failed to shape the overarching relationship between the two countries. The cultural balance shifted after the war. In the 1920s, American tourism in Europe increased dramatically: travel in Europe shifted from an elite phenomenon to an upper-middle-class commonplace event. American industrial technology inspired both admiration and fear across the Atlantic. American domination of new popular media such as film drew both large European audiences and calls for cultural protection. (The warning of a London newspaper—"The film is to America what the flag was once to Britain. By its means Uncle Sam may hope some day, if he be not checked in time, to Americanize the world"—might have been uttered by Jack Lang, until recently France's minister of culture.[46]) In an era of supposed isolation, the American giant seemed everywhere in Europe.

Ironically, this cultural invasion was accompanied by the persistence of "pervasive ignorance" on either side of the Atlantic. Former French Minister of Culture David Reynolds documents the resilience of outdated images that Britain and the United States held of each other, even though the two did not confront a language barrier. The United States remained inaccessible to most of the European population apart from a small elite, and even elite contacts in the United States were typically a very narrow and unrepresentative slice of American society. The popularity of American culture only reinforced distorted popular images of the United States such as the movie portrait of gangsters and crime. The American viewpoint was equally skewed: obsessed with the British class system, Americans widely believed that "Britain was not a genuine democracy."[47] Although popular culture made it impossible for Europeans to ignore the United States, the new media had not become, on the eve of World War II, an avenue of enhanced transparency or understanding on either side of the Atlantic.

5. REVISION AND PREVISION: HISTORY AND THE TRANSATLANTIC FUTURE

In his discussion of the power of historical analogy, Yuen Foong Khong warns that "when the lessons [of historical analogies] become part of the unspoken and spoken lore, when there is only one consensual interpretation, their premises and their relevance become matters of dogma that few will see fit to question. At that point, analogies step beyond their roles as heuristic devices for discovering facts and explanations and assume the roles of explanations and facts themselves."[48] The internationalist narrative of transatlantic relations in this century has become a part of the "lore" of American foreign policy, helping to sustain American involvement in and commitment to Europe during the Cold War. A reexamination of that narrative in light of recent historical scholarship, however, undermines it and reintroduces an element of contestation in its monolithic and heroic image of American policy. In place of its emphasis on threat-induced ruptures in American relations with Europe, transatlantic ties are better seen, as Neustadt and May recommend, as a continuous stream of engagement between the United States and Europe across the decades. After the United States achieved the status of a major industrial power in the late nineteenth century, genuine isolation from Europe became virtually impossible. The rapid expansion of the United States overseas meant imperial clashes with the Europeans. Even when convinced of relative security behind their oceanic barriers, American elites were preoccupied with European military and ideological threats to the hemisphere. When this history is combined with modern military technology, enhanced transportation and communications capabilities, and cultural melding, any current toying with a full-fledged retreat across the Atlantic borders on the fantastic.

Undermining a dominant image of the transatlantic past that is based on a single determinant—military threat—opens the way for alternative readings of the past and broadened speculation about the future. At the same time, embracing a more variegated past leaves unsettled the degree to which that past may resemble the future. Using the technique of likenesses and differences that Neustadt and May suggest, the transatlantic past can be revealed as either another, very distant world with little applicability to the future, or as a familiar landscape rich in historical similarities to our post–Cold War future.

Many of the differences between transatlantic relations in the earlier decades and our own immediate future point toward less volatility and less conflict, contrary to predictions based on the internationalist myth: a shared aversion to imperialism and intervention, parallel views on the organization of the international economy, the spread of democracy in Europe, and the proliferation of international institutions. The United States first confronted the European powers in the course of competing for influence in Asia, Latin America, and other spheres of imperial expansion. These "out-of-area" rivalries played a prominent role in the first decades of NATO as the European powers resisted United States pressure to speed decolonization. Even when the Soviet threat was at its peak, the history of NATO was littered with sharp disputes over European and American initiatives outside Europe—Palestine, Indonesia, Suez, Vietnam, the Middle East. That field of rivalry has now virtually disappeared: as recent events in Somalia and Haiti suggest, we may be entering an age of anti-imperialism, in which the great powers lack political support or a clear-cut set of interests for intervention in third areas. Although the Bosnian conflict has produced sharp conflict between the United States and its NATO allies, it is not conflict of the classical imperial variety, but clashes over assuming responsibility for an unwanted peacekeeping role.

The dissipation of this sphere of competition between the United States and Europe, the end of imperial ambitions, has also affected a second key dimension in transatlantic ties: economic collaboration and conflict. Despite predictions of new economic warfare among the major industrial powers (including Europe and the United States), economic rivalries are likely to be far less intense than in previous periods. In the past, economic rivalry between the United States and its allies was unremitting, even during times of high external threat (such as World War II). Much of that conflict was driven by fundamentally different conceptions of world economic order. The United States, distrustful of discriminatory, bilaterally negotiated imperial spheres, while the British and the French were determined to maintain their protected economic spaces against the American economic behemoth. Over the last century underlying agreement between the United States and Europe on the outlines of the world economy has seldom been greater, whatever the current state of bargaining within the General Agreement on Tariffs and Trade or the Group of Seven. European politics no longer awards power to economic nationalists that propose a fundamentally different world economic order; alternatives of protection and closure on the political left are also weak. Although this difference with the past does not foreclose continued economic conflict, the stakes in that conflict are very different.

Pessimists point to regional projects in Europe and North America as the equivalents of old imperial blocs and the source of future economic conflict. Successive extensions of the European Community and its discriminatory trading arrangements have inspired complaints from the United States and other trading partners; East Asian producers have criticized provisions of the North American Free Trade Agreement as well. Leaving aside the important question of whether the world economy is becoming more regionalized (outside the European Community this is uncertain), simplistic parallels between current regional arrangements and the neomercantilist blocs of the 1930s are an abuse of history on a grand scale. The impulse in contemporary trading blocs is both liberalizing and somewhat discriminatory. Old-style blocs were blatantly protectionist and highly discriminatory; they required tight government controls over most external transactions—goods, foreign exchange, investment. Existing trading blocs have removed or reduced such government interventions. Nor have the contemporary regional arrangements inspired high levels of conflict: American fears of "Fortress Europe" were in general belied by the consequences of the Single European Act. NAFTA is hardly a threat to European firms that are actively investing in the United States to profit from the North American market. Apart from the European Union, regional arrangements have not demonstrated the need or the desire for rapid institution-building. In any case, the implications of regionalization for transatlantic collaboration remain ambiguous. Strong regional entities could produce greater competence for collaboration at the global level. Regionalization may exact a price, but its price is likely to be one of distraction from transatlantic and global concerns, reinforcing the inward-looking tendencies in European and American domestic politics.

The alignment of American and European preferences in the international economy has been deepened by an even more important transformation: the spread of democracy in Europe. It is difficult to imagine the beleaguered position of the United States, Britain, and France in 1940, when democratic partners in Europe were so few. As Samuel Huntington notes, the 1920s and 1930s were times of democratic reversals; only four of the countries (most of them European) that became democracies between 1910 and 1931 remained democratic during the interwar decades.[49] Comprehending appeasement during the 1930s demands an understanding that democracy was not seen as the wave of the future before World War II, but appeared as a threatened, rare, and fragile political form.

Western and Central Europe are now solidly democratic; since the 1970s, Mediterranean Europe has also joined the ranks of stable democracies. Much has been made of the low probability of war among democratic states. More significant for the day-to-day collaborative efforts that comprise transatlantic relations is the higher level of transparency among democracies regarding domestic politics and national preferences. Predictability and trust are far more likely to flourish in a context of democratic regimes. Misperception, born of apparent rather than real familiarity, is certainly possible, but the consequences of misperceptions are likely to be less grave and long-lasting between democratic partners.

A final difference with the pre-1940 era is equally important: the proliferation of international institutions and other, more ad hoc channels of contact between the United States and Europe. The era of international conferences was born before 1914, and functional international organizations dealing with the consequences of growing economic integration had emerged in the nineteenth century, but the scale and intensity of transatlantic consultation across a wide range of issues is now many times greater than it was in the 1920s and 1930s. Louis Rasminsky, a Canadian who worked as secretary to the Financial Committee of the League of Nations and was a founder of the Bretton Woods organizations, noted that "the difference in the amount and the character of consultation is spectacular. Before the war, there was great diffidence about discussing anybody's domestic economic policies or the impact of those policies on other countries' positions, and discussion tended to be focused exclusively on 'external' economic policy such as tariff barriers."[50]

Each of these differences with the pre–Cold War decades argues for much more stability in the stream of transatlantic history than the internationalist narrative would allow. With the disappearance of the Soviet threat, however, those predicting more transatlantic conflict have emphasized other differences between the United States and Europe. Closer economic integration may produce novel forms of conflict. The newest form is system friction between different variants of capitalism—differences that are sometimes painted in colors as vivid as the old differences between the democratic West and the communist East. Most attention is devoted to the Japanese (or East Asian) variant of capitalism and the ways in which it does or does not function like Western (North American and European) capitalism and does or does not converge on an established Western model of political economy. Others, however, detect a European or German model of capitalism as well, one that is pitted against the more market-oriented, less-interventionist model prevalent in the United States.[51] As the industrialized economies become more tightly integrated, previously insignificant domestic differences become the source of outside scrutiny and international economic conflict, whether it is European subsidies to agriculture and aerospace or the Japanese distribution system. Those who are most alarmist about these conflicts among political economies are also skeptical that existing international institutions and forums provide a means for resolving them or that new mechanisms can be constructed to do so. Although the industrialized economies on either side of the Atlantic appear more homogeneous than they did in 1940, demands for harmonization of national systems have been heightened as the volume of trade and investment has increased.

Apart from the unresolved issue of system differences and the potential that it poses for future economic conflict, other differences and similarities that emerge when the post–Cold War Atlantic relationship is compared with earlier eras provide less clear-cut predictions of the future. One legacy of the Cold War and the internationalist narrative is a belief that the pattern of transatlantic relations has been driven overwhelmingly by American policy: the desire of Europeans for American involvement and security guarantees was believed to be relatively constant. Any examination of recent scholarship casts considerable doubt on that assumption. Even the formation of NATO, according to recent research, resulted more from British initiatives than from American prodding.[52] In the future, even more than in the past, the attitude of the Europeans toward American engagement will be a critical determinant of the shape of transatlantic relations. The European stance, in turn, will be shaped by the progress of European integration and institution-building: if the European Community—a tremendous break with the pre-1945 pattern of intra-European relations—proceeds to construct a common currency and central bank and can be taken seriously as a single military and diplomatic entity, then the desire for American engagement in Europe is likely to decline. To the degree that those processes falter, as they have recently, the desire for continued and close collaboration with the United States will persist. On the present stop-and-go pattern of European integration, one can imagine that European attitudes will resemble those of the 1920s, another period of diffuse security threats, when European elites wanted "to co-opt the United States but did not want the United States to be the supreme arbiter of their affairs."[53]

Another imponderable difference is the changed position of the transatlantic relationship within the global system. Whatever the balance between Europe and the United States in earlier periods, there was little question that together Western Europe and the United States dominated the world economy and set the outlines of international politics. That dominance is confirmed by the fact that two European civil wars are customarily labeled "world wars." Although the weight of Europe and the United States in the contemporary international order should not be undervalued, other players outside the Atlantic orbit have necessarily assumed a more prominent place and claim a share of the attention and cooperative initiatives that used to be directed exclusively across the Atlantic. For the United States, the Pacific region has assumed a position in its foreign policy that correlates closely with its remarkable rate of economic growth and its trading prowess. For Western Europe, the stability and integration of Central and Eastern Europe have become major preoccupations. But these foreign policy alternatives are not simply objects of attention; they are actors, and their foreign policies on global issues—military, economic, environmental—will alter the terms of bargaining between the United States and Europe in ways as yet unforeseen. To cite only one example, the willingness of Japan to assume additional international economic and military roles would almost certainly relieve some of the tension over burden-sharing that is likely to plague relations between the United States and Europe. Or one could imagine a future democratic Russia that plays on differences between the United States and Europe in a much more calculated and successful way than the old Soviet regime. The strategic interaction between Europe and the United States will be increasingly and unpredictably influenced by the actions, calculated and unwitting, of other players in the system.

A final historical regularity will also reappear to work its effects on the transatlantic relationship of the future: the tug of domestic political demands. The period of greatest transatlantic estrangement in this century was undoubtedly the Great Depression, when American and European politics were overwhelmed by demands for economic recovery. Those were the years when Herbert Hoover could convince himself that the United States could recover "independently of what may happen elsewhere." The first years of the Wilson administration, when the progressive movement reached its peak in the United States and an agenda of domestic reform dominated American politics, were another period of relative disengagement from European affairs. Even allowing for the cyclical concentration in domestic economic issues that accompanies recessions, the industrialized countries appear to have entered another period of domestic absorption. After years of claiming that the line between foreign and domestic policy is increasingly blurred, the American foreign policy elite has joined the chorus of those urging America to take a break from international responsibilities, to turn inward and devote more time and attention to its domestic ills. Calculating the effects of such a shift in orientation (if it can persist) is difficult, but given the pull of domestic demands during even the most internationalist eras, its effect on transatlantic ties may be substantial.

Another trend in domestic politics on either side of the Atlantic could be even more important: the gradual erosion of internationalism on both the right and the left of the political spectrum. American isolationism in the 1920s and 1930s was a political force that drew on both progressives and diehard Republican conservatives. It also found support in ethnic groups that opposed particular European allies and in a general anxiety over the effect of foreign entanglements on an ethnically diverse society.[54] In the 1990s it is not clear the internationalist center of American foreign policy will hold indefinitely. Opponents of internationalism have used the end of the Cold War to question international engagements of all kinds. The debate over NAFTA became a climactic battle between economic nationalists and internationalists, despite the relative insignificance of the agreement for the American economy. The agreement was assailed by labor and environmentalists on the left and nationalists such as Ross Perot and

Pat Buchanan on the right. In similar fashion, the World Bank and the International Monetary Fund have come under attack from the same unusual alliance of conservative and left-wing interest groups. Anti-intervention has become a central theme of the Republican Party since the G.O.P. took control of the U.S. Congress in 1995. Whether undermining of the internationalist myth will strengthen these newly aroused political forces is a central question of American foreign policy in the 1990s.

In Europe, nationalism has also strengthened in at least some countries: the Berlusconi coalition in Italy (the first postwar coalition to include neo-fascists), the eruption of anti-European factionalism in the British Conservative Party, and the surge in support for an anti-immigrant party in Austria could be bellwethers of a shift toward nationalist sentiment. If that trend affects the larger European countries, it could undermine both the European Union and the transatlantic alliance.

6. CONCLUSION: HISTORICAL REVISION AND TRANSATLANTIC CHANGE

The collapse of the Soviet empire and the end of the Cold War are only the most dramatic changes, international and domestic, that may create stresses for a transatlantic relationship built in another time for different purposes. Nevertheless, those events did begin an undermining of the internationalist myth that had supported the Cold War transatlantic relationship since 1945. A more nuanced, and perhaps less politically appealing, account of the transatlantic past may be required to sustain a cooperative future that is as successful as the last half century. In place of a narrative based on realist precepts that grounds American involvement in Europe solely in a common and pressing military threat, a liberal recounting could offer a portrait of more sustained engagement based on economic, cultural, and ideological ties as well as military ones. Rather than a simple prediction of "back to the (multipolar) future," such a reinterpretation would emphasize a "ratchet effect" in transatlantic relations that will prevent any simple return to the past of a century or half-century ago. Five decades of close collaboration have produced societies on either side of the Atlantic that share broadly common views on domestic political ordering and international economic governance, societies that are deeply engaged in a dense network of institutional ties. Imponderables remain, of course: the foreign policy choices that a more unified and self-confident Europe might make, the uncertain effects of the relative decline of the Atlantic economy within the international system, and, above all, the vagaries of domestic political change.

The sorry story of the collapse of both the gold standard and international cooperation during the Depression offers an important final caution in present circumstances: clinging to an outdated and insupportable framework for cooperation may be the worst possible response to altered circumstances. Since many of the differences between probable futures and the transatlantic past appear to lower contemporary obstacles to collaboration, the dense and formal character of existing structures of collaboration may not be required to sustain a cooperative transatlantic relationship. Nor does cooperation need to be intensified in every forum to arrest a backward slide into nationalist hostility. Given positive changes in the international security environment, NATO may no longer be the optimal means for collaborating on security issues of joint concern. Although Europe and the United States should not lightly discard an institutional framework that has taken years to construct, the history of the gold standard suggests that a particular *form* of cooperation should not be taken to symbolize the *fact* of cooperation. The stream of transatlantic history has broad banks, and it has run deeper with each succeeding decade. The new past unearthed by historians is not the past feared by internationalist alarmists or embraced by those nostalgic for an unencumbered (and insecure) place in the world. In any case, returning to that past is the least likely of many possible transatlantic futures.

NOTES

1. Ernest R. May, *Lessons of the Past: The Use and Misuse of History in American Foreign Policy* (London: Oxford University Press, 1973); Richard E. Neustadt and Ernest R. May, *Thinking in Time: The Uses of History for Decision-Makers* (New York: The Free Press, 1986); and Yuen Foong Khong, *Analogies at War* (Princeton: Princeton University Press, 1992).
2. A striking example of bad history put to good use (at least in the eyes of economic liberals) occurred during debate over the North American Free Trade Agreement (NAFTA), with the mobilization of the Smoot-Hawley Tariff and the memories of the Great Depression. The analogy between opposition to

NAFTA and the protectionism of Smoot-Hawley seemed strained to many, but the memory still resonated.

3. See, for example, Stephen Walt, *The Origins of Alliances* (Ithaca: Cornell University Press, 1987). Walt writes: "Although NATO's elaborate institutional structure will slow the pace of devolution, only a resurgence of the Soviet threat is likely to preserve NATO in anything like its present form" (p. vii).
4. John Mearsheimer, "Back to the Future: Instability in Europe after the Cold War," *International Security,* vol. 15, no. 1 (Summer 1990), pp. 5–56.
5. James Schlesinger, "The Transatlantic Partnership: An American View," *Brookings Review*, vol. 10, no. 3 (Summer 1992), pp. 17–21.
6. Christopher Layne and Benjamin Schwartz, "American Hegemony—Without an Enemy," *Foreign Policy*, vol. 92 (Fall 1993), pp. 5–23.
7. Owen Harries, "The Collapse of 'The West,'" *Foreign Affairs*, vol. 72, no. 4 (September/October 1993), p. 50.
8. Lester Thurow, *Head to Head: The Coming Economic Battle among Japan, Europe, and America* (New York: Morrow, 1992).
9. Jeffrey Garten, *A Cold Peace: America, Japan, Germany, and the Struggle for Supremacy* (New York: Times Books, 1992), p. 45.
10. Wayne Sandholtz et al., *The Highest Stakes: The Economic Foundations of the Next Security System* (New York: Oxford University Press, 1992), pp. 197–99.
11. On American concerns over German designs in the hemisphere, see Hans Gatzke, *Germany and the United States: A "Special Relationship?"* (Cambridge: Harvard University Press, 1980), pp. 49, 122; and Manfred Jonas, *The United States and Germany: A Diplomatic History* (Ithaca, New York: Cornell University Press, 1984), p. 68.
12. Paul M. Kennedy, *The Samoan Tangle: A Study in Anglo-German-American Relations, 1878–1900* (New York: Harper & Row, 1974), p. 133.
13. Ibid., p. 137.
14. Paul M. Kennedy, "British and American Reactions to the Rise of American Power," in R. J. Bullen, H. Pogge Von Strandmann, and A. B. Polonsky, eds., *Ideas into Politics: Aspects of European History, 1880–1900* (London: Croom Helm, 1984), p. 17.
15. Ernest R. May, *Imperial Democracy: The Emergence of America as a Great Power* (New York: Harcourt, Brace & World, 1961), pp. 44–45 and 54–55.
16. Kennedy, *The Samoan Tangle*, p. 291.
17. On this record, see May, *Imperial Democracy*; and Edward P. Crapol, "From Anglophobia to Fragile Rapprochement: Anglo-American Relations in the Early Twentieth Century," in H.-J. Schröder, ed., *Confrontation and Cooperation: Germany and the United States in the Era of World War I, 1900–1924* (Providence: Berg Publishers, 1993), pp. 13–31.

18. Paul M. Kennedy, "British and American Reactions to the Rise of American Power," in Bullen, Pogge Von Strandmann, and Polonsky, *Ideas into Politics*, p. 20.
19. Cited in Jonas, *The United States and Germany*, p. 80.
20. Peter Krüger, "German Disappointment and Anti-Western Resentment, 1918–1919," in Schröder, *Confrontation and Cooperation*, p. 333. On the hostility of the German press and reports on its hostility in the United States, see Gatzke, *Germany and the United States*, p. 48.
21. Walter Lippmann, "Rough-Hew Them How We Will," *Foreign Affairs*, vol. 15, no. 4 (July 1937), p. 593.
22. On the issue of whether Germany and the United States were world powers before 1914, see Ragnhild Fiebig-von Hase, "The United States and Germany in the World Arena, 1900–1917," in Schröder, *Confrontation and Cooperation*, pp. 33–68.
23. "Discussion," in Schröder *Confrontation and Cooperation*, p. 419.
24. Brian McKercher, "Reaching for the Brass Ring: The Recent Historiography of Interwar American Foreign Relations," *Diplomatic History*, vol. 15, no. 4 (Fall 1991), pp. 565–98.
25. Jonas, *The United States and Germany*, p. 154; compare Leffler's characterization that the United States sought "a framework designed to maximize America's financial leverage and minimize her strategic commitments," in Melvyn P. Leffler, *The Elusive Quest* (Chapel Hill: University of North Carolina Press, 1979).
26. Speech at New Haven, December 29, 1922, cited in Jonas, *The United States and Germany*, pp. 171–72.
27. Frank Costigliola, *Awkward Dominion: American Political, Economic, and Cultural Relations with Europe, 1919–1933* (Ithaca: Cornell University Press, 1984), p. 67.
28. Stephen A. Schuker, "Origins of American Stabilization Policy in Europe: The Financial Dimension, 1918–1924," in Schröder, *Confrontation and Cooperation*, p. 377.
29. Ibid., pp. 391–92.
30. Jonas, *The United States and Germany*, pp. 171–72; and Costigliola, *Awkward Dominion*, pp. 62–63.
31. Costigliola, *Awkward Dominion*, p. 17.
32. Ibid., p. 112.
33. Leffler, *Elusive Quest*, pp. 116–17.
34. Ibid., p. 158.
35. Michael Hogan, *Informal Entente: The Private Structure of Cooperation in Anglo-American Economic Diplomacy, 1918–1928* (Columbia, MO: University of Missouri Press, 1977).
36. This was particularly clear in the sphere of communications. Ibid., ch. 6.

37. See McKercher, "Reaching for the Brass Ring," pp. 585–87; and ———, "Wealth, Power, and the New International Order: Britain and the American Challenge in the 1920s," *Diplomatic History*, vol. 12, no. 4 (Fall 1988), pp. 411–42.
38. Put most powerfully by Charles Kindleberger, *The World in Depression: 1929–1939* (London: Allen Lane, 1973).
39. Costigliola, *Awkward Dominion*, p. 16.
40. Barry Eichengreen, *Golden Fetters: The Gold Standard and the Great Depression, 1919–1939* (New York: Oxford University Press, 1992), p. 4; also "The Gold-Exchange Standard and the Great Depression," in Barry Eichengreen, *Elusive Stability: Essays in the History of International Finance, 1919–1939*, (Cambridge: Cambridge University Press, 1990) pp. 239–70.
41. Eichengreen, "The Gold-Exchange Standard and The Great Depression," p. 394.
42. In addition to Eichengreen's detailed account, parallel arguments are made by Peter Temin, *Lessons from the Great Depression: The Lionel Robbins Lectures for 1989* (Cambridge: MIT Press, 1989), ch. 1.
43. Leffler, *Elusive Quest*, p. 202.
44. McKercher, "Wealth, Power, and the New International Order, pp. 411–12."
45. Jonas, *The United States and Germany*, pp. 227 and 232.
46. Costigliola, *Awkward Dominion*, pp. 21, 173, and 177.
47. David Reynolds, *The Creation of the Anglo-American Alliance 1437–41: A Study in Competitive Cooperation* (London: Europa Publication, 1981), pp. 11–13 and 23.
48. Khong, *Analogies at War*, p. 262.
49. Samuel P. Huntington, *The Third Wave: Democratization in the Late Twentieth Century* (Norman, OK: University of Oklahoma Press, 1991), p. 17.
50. Louis Rasminsky in A. L. K. Acheson, J. F. Chant, and M. F. J. Prachowny, eds., *Bretton Woods Revisited* (Toronto: University of Toronto Press, 1972), p. 37.
51. This is one theme of Garten, *A Cold Peace*; see also Michel Albert, *Capitalism against Capitalism* (London: Whurr, 1993).
52. Martin H. Folly, "Breaking the Vicious Circle: Britain, the United States, and the Genesis of the North Atlantic Treaty," *Diplomatic History*, vol. 12, no. 1 (Winter 1988), pp. 59–77.
53. Manfred Berg, "Trade, Debts, and Reparations: Economic Concepts and Political Constraints," in Schröder, *Confrontation and Cooperation*, p. 413.
54. Lippmann, "Rough-Hew Them How We Will," pp. 590–91.

Historical Continuity and Discontinuity in Transatlantic Relations: Consequences for the Future

Werner Link

1. INTRODUCTION

The profound changes that have been taking place in the international system since 1989 have given rise to a feeling of insecurity in both America and Europe. In particular, there is insecurity regarding the future of transatlantic relations, which, as part of the international system, will be affected by those changes that are now occurring. As is always the case in times of transition—when old structures give way to new ones—we attempt to ascertain the maintenance of certain elements of continuity. Furthermore, the feeling of discontinuity and instability prompts us to look for continuity and seek renewed stability. Thus continuity in the historical and political process—and, indeed, continuity in the midst of change—has advanced to become the central issue in political life and in the political science debate.

But what exactly do we mean when we talk about continuity in the political and social process in general, and transatlantic relations in particular? There is no generally accepted definition or even theory of continuity in the social sciences, although there are certainly some useful heuristic starting points. With reference to the ideas of the American economist Alexander Gerschenkron, continuity will be construed as the recurrence of similar situations or constellations in international politics and as a directional constant of foreign policy actions.[1] In other words, in the situational sphere of international politics, continuity occurs when similar or similarly structured situations recur at different periods; and in the conceptual and operational sphere of foreign policy, continuity is perceivable when intended or real action moves in the same or in a similar direction.

In international relations theory these interconnected spheres have been discussed repeatedly. The theory of structural realism (also known as neo-realism) has demonstrated clearly that although states determine their foreign policy on the basis of their internal structure and in accordance with their internal decision-making processes, the structure and constraints of the international system and their position within the community of states is just as important. "[I]ts decisions are shaped by the very presence of other states as well as by interactions with them. When and how internal forces find external expression, if they do, cannot be explained in terms of the interacting parties if the situation in which they act and interact constrains them from some actions, disposes them toward others, and affects the outcomes of their interactions."[2] If one accepts this approach, then it is clear that similarly structured international situations can lead to similar problems and point foreign policy in a similar direction.

Taken to its logical conclusion, this leads to the balance-of-power theorem that was developed in the theory of statecraft over the centuries,[3] and to its modern equivalent, structural realism.[4] Proceeding from the assumption that states strive for security—that is, self-preservation and self-fulfillment—and this in the context of the decentralized and quasi-anarchical system of states, the central hypothesis follows: under conditions of a self-help system, the threat posed by a great power leads the threatened state to a policy of counterweight formation (that is, to a policy of balancing), and from a common threat situation there emanates the tendency to form a common counterweight (that is, alliances). Furthermore, both the threat and the formation of a counterweight can be either comprehensive or sector-specific (that is, military, economic, and cultural). Thus changes in the distribution of power and in the threat situation lead to recurring patterns in the arrangement of the states concerned. A cooperative balance of power (or concert of powers) exists only as long as no single power or grouping of states threatens to predominate. If this is not the case, there will be an antagonistic balance of power. Every balance-of-power system is more or less unstable as a result, among other things, of the fact that great powers always try to be slightly stronger than their rivals (and this is often linked with striving for hegemony).[5]

When applying these general ideas to transatlantic relations, one obviously needs to remember that in addition to governments, social actors are engaged in action and interaction, and therefore what are known as transnational relations should not be overlooked.[6] Furthermore, it is important to note that unlike the United States, Europe does not form a single state. The differences in the various arrangements between the European states were and continue to be a crucial element in the development of the transatlantic arrangement. As to the United States, until the beginning of the twentieth century, it did not form part of the system of the European great powers, in which the issue of "balance or hegemony" arose repeatedly—an issue that was a fundamental problem, succinctly described by the German historian Ludwig Dehio.[7] At this time transatlantic relations were determined more by ideological, intellectual, and sociocultural conflicts than by questions of political power. However, the more it became apparent—and, indeed, the more it was anticipated—that the United States would become a great power, the more pressing became the question of how the United States would fit into the concert of powers, and of what shape the relationship between Europe and the United States could or should assume. As we shall see, the alternatives became clear, and they continued to play a role after the United States became a member (for good, after it entered the war in 1917) of what was now the globalized system of great powers. Thereby, for better or for worse, it became part of the dialectic of the striving for hegemony and the formation of countervailing power.

What consequences did this have for transatlantic relations? How did the changes in the balance of power in Europe and between the European states and the United States determine both change and continuity? Have similar threat situations led to similar arrangements in the formation of a countervailing power, and after the disappearance of the threats, were there similar or different points of departure and problems of redefinition—with similar or different paths and patterns of action in the transatlantic relationship? And finally, what are the consequences for the present and the future?[8]

These questions are at the center of the following analysis. Appropriately, it begins with a brief account of the alternative concepts and tendencies that evolved in the course of the nineteenth century and became important, in a variety of ways, for transatlantic relations in the twentieth century.

2. TENDENCIES AND ALTERNATIVE CONCEPTS IN THE NINETEENTH CENTURY

Shared transatlantic values at first did not exist; rather, transatlantic relations initially were characterized by disagreement over values. The original vision of the American Founding Fathers, which was to be a "city on the hill" and thus illuminate the world, was retained when the United States came into being.[9] It was "to give to mankind the magnanimous and too novel example of a people always guided by an exalted justice and benevolence."[10] This exceptional case acquired a missionary quality because the American model was deemed to possess universal validity, especially when it was compared with Europe and its rival and egoistical powers. However, initially this missionary zeal did not involve an outward display of power.

Thus America "played a role in European life as an idea before America began to be of interest to Europe as an actual power factor."[11] Furthermore, in the nineteenth century this dynamic was marked by two contrasting processes that continued to be operative in the twentieth century: the "repression" and the "discovery" of America in the European consciousness.[12]

Of crucial importance for the repression, or exclusion, of America was the fact that the American Revolution was soon overshadowed by the French Revolution, which replaced it as a political model. Yet at the same time, the "discovery" of America made the new state and its social structure seem both a refuge and an anticipation of the future of Europe. Insofar as America was seen to be a refuge, that perception led to the mass exodus of parts of the European underclass, and the flight or emigration of those persecuted for political and religious reasons. They went to the United States because it was the land of unlimited opportunity and freedom. The numbers involved reflect the ups and downs of economic and political developments in Europe, and reached an annual maximum of about one million in some years before the First World War. In 1924 a new quota system came into force, gradually putting to an end uncontrolled European immigration.

Of greater significance for European intellectual interaction with America was the discovery of America in terms of its anticipation of the future of Europe—that is, the discovery that America and its social and political culture constituted a different model—"la contre-partie sociale du continent européen," as the Abbé de Pradt wrote in 1824 in *L'Europe et l'Amérique en 1822 et 1823*.[13] Similarly, in 1835 Alexis de Tocqueville perceived America to be a society in which the guiding principle was democratic equality. The discovery of this basic quality, which was contrasted with the political and social conditions that prevailed in Europe, was linked to the assumption that it anticipated the future of Europe, "that, sooner or later, we shall arrive like the Americans, at an almost complete equality of condition."[14] This was a revolutionary perspective as far as Europe was concerned, and it raised both hopes and fears. European liberals, especially in the revolutions of 1848, eagerly seized on such ideas, espousing them with enthusiasm and a great deal of fervor. They even hoped that American democracy would intervene on the side of European liberalism in the sense of "systemic support."[15] The maxim of the liberal revolutionaries in Europe was "you must interfere if you want to avoid being interfered with."[16] This was not as yet the American maxim, although the notion of a transatlantic value community based on the idea of liberal democracy had taken root. In the twentieth century it was destined to receive more than token support in the United States.

The political and sociostructural differences between Europe and the United States were felt even more strongly (on both sides of the Atlantic) in the aftermath of the restoration of the old order. Thus the transatlantic distance remained. Thereafter, the "Americanization" of Europe predicted by de Tocqueville, which now began to assume concrete form, was accompanied by the emergence of positive and negative European reactions. Europe's sociocultural interaction with America began to be increasingly characterized by Americanization and anti-Americanism, which were two sides of the same coin.

These dialectical processes of the repression and the discovery of America that were discernible in the ideological and sociocultural sphere also existed in the sphere of power politics. Here it is also possible to discern, on the one hand, the repression of America, the disastrous effects of which first came fully into view in the twentieth century, and, on the other hand, the discovery of the United States as a power factor, which was linked with an anticipation and a premonition of America's geopolitical role.

As to that aspect, it suffices to recall de Tocqueville's assessments and the conclusions that he drew from the size of the territory and the population, from the geostrategic position of the union, and from the national significance of trade. These led him to surmise that the United States would "one day become the foremost maritime power of the globe," and that no commercial power "can be durable if it cannot be united, in case of need, to naval force."[17] De Tocqueville's expectations finally culminated in the famous comparison between the United States and Russia.[18]

The literature on the subject demonstrates in detail that this comparison was typical of contemporary thinking in Europe and America. It was the origin of the bipolar view of the world, which saw a dual challenge to Europe from Russia and the United States, and thereby superseded Eurocentric patterns of thought. Thus in 1855, influenced by the Crimean War, the German left-wing democrat Julius Fröbel wrote from his American exile "that a global balance of political power is beginning to replace the European balance of political power. High-level politics have become global politics. . . . America and Russia have become the two poles of the political world, and between them lies western Europe as a transitional center."[19]

As a rule such analyses of political power were closely linked to an ideological attitude that was based on the polarity between freedom and despotism, or between despotism in the east and liberal democracy in the west. It is of interest to note that a similar interpretation was also favored by those writers in the United States who, like their European colleagues, saw their country and Russia as the future poles of global politics.[20]

All this was not without significance for the conceptual organization of Europe and for the possible patterns of transatlantic relations. The majority of the variants that were discussed repeatedly and in part implemented in the twentieth century were already in existence in the nineteenth century, at least in a rudimentary form.[21] Others appeared at a later stage:

(1) Europe together with America as a counterpoise against the threat of an expansionist and despotically governed Russia—in other words, a transatlantic alliance between (western/central) Europe and the United States against tsarist Russia, and later against Bolshevik Russia (the bipolar concept);

(2) A continental bloc in the shape of an alliance between Germany and Russia against the United States and Britain (the dual concept of a continental system against another system, land power against naval power);

(3) Europe as a third global power next to the United States and Russia in the shape of cooperation between or a federation of the European states, and in the context of mutual restraint and cooperation, as long as none of the parties threatened to become predominant (the triangular concept);

(4) Central Europe as a unified economic area and as a political federation under German or Austro-German leadership (a geographically delimited version of the second or third concept).

From a European point of view, all these concepts were based on the common problem of how to arrest the decline of Europe in the face of the rise of the United States and Russia. Of crucial importance for the relationship between Europe and America was whether and which European states would be willing to organize their relations by means of cooperation or federation. Without such cooperation or federation, even the closest transatlantic relationship would have been characterized by an asymmetry between the United States and the European powers of such magnitude that the United States would have had to function as a hegemonic power or balancer (as Britain had once done) in order to avert the global hegemony of Russia.

The situation around the turn of the century was complicated and fundamentally altered by the fact that a new great power, Germany, was perceived to be a hegemonic threat to the other European great powers *and* to the emerging world powers, the United States and Russia. The transatlantic coalition of the First World War was a reaction to this situation. However, it was not directed against Russia (as originally envisaged in concept 1), but against Germany and its striving for world power.[22] The coalition included Russia. In a way this coalition was a variant of the bipolar concept created in the laboratory of history, and it was to be repeated in the Second World War.

3. THE ORIGINS OF THE FIRST TRANSATLANTIC WAR COALITION

It was neither predictable nor inevitable that the grouping that led to the First World War coalition should have come about the way it did. However, the economic rise of the United States was predictable and unmistakable.[23] Around the turn of the century the "city on the hill," which had arisen in the New World in opposition to Europe, and which soon began to have a global influence, became a center of heavy industry and, indeed, a "factory on a hill."[24] Europe began to be haunted by the specter of the "Americanization of the world," fearing not democratic ideas, but

American goods.[25] One American commentator proudly proclaimed: "Commercially we are breaking into every market in the world. It is part of our development. We are marching fast to the economic supremacy of the world."[26] As de Tocqueville had predicted, in the last decade of the nineteenth century the U.S. government made strenuous efforts to increase the size of the U.S. Navy, a policy strongly influenced by Alfred Thayer Mahan's 1890 book *The Influence of Sea Power upon History*, in which commercial, missionary, and political factors were combined in a specifically American concept of imperialism.[27]

This is not the place to describe the various shades of imperialist and anti-imperialist opinion in the United States around the turn of the century.[28] Mainstream American global strategy came to be characterized by the Open Door Policy, the idea that free access to markets was the most suitable method of protecting American interests on a global basis. As President William Taft put it in 1912, it was a matter of "substituting dollars for bullets."[29] Whereas skeptics had been of the opinion—before the American colonies achieved independence—that America was "formed for happiness, but not for empire," it was no longer a contradiction.[30] The spread of "the American dream" occurred under the aegis of a middle-class striving for property and happiness that was based on the idea of peaceful expansion. Its maxim was "no longer war but trade," and it sought to spread technical progress and democracy with the help of the "diplomacy of peace." "Americanism against imperialism" signified a preference for a kind of "informal imperialism," an informal empire based on American trade and the export of American culture.[31]

The global power structure that gave political meaning to George Washington's maxim not to enter into alliances that constricted America's room for maneuver was conveniently repressed in public opinion. However, farsighted politicians and journalists who thought in terms of realpolitik were fully aware that America had developed in the shadow of the balance of power maintained by Britain, and that the United States would increasingly have to make an active contribution to global stability.[32]

America was particularly interested in maintaining the European balance of power and preventing the hegemony of the German empire. This became an important feature of American foreign policy even before the outbreak of the First World War, and formed the basis of significant interests that coincided with those of Britain and France. It assumed a number of forms in terms of practical politics, and differed from the various constellations during the crises that characterized these decades, and from the politics of the European powers.[33]

As earlier research on the subject has demonstrated, there were several U.S.-German "attempts at harmonization."[34] However, the differences between the two countries in political, economic, and intellectual terms were profound. The German concept was to create a central European bloc under German leadership, an idea that was first pursued at the time of Chancellor Leo Graf von Caprivi (1890–94) and once again came to dominate German political thinking during the First World War.[35] This continental bloc in the long term, was to be directed against the United States, Russia, and the British empire, in order to meet the American challenge.

It was "extremely paradoxical" that mistrust of the German empire's intentions should have grown precisely in those phases of the prewar era in which German policy had turned away from Caprivi's central Europe concept and was being more accommodating toward American interests (for example, in the area of customs and excise policies).[36] Yet President Woodrow Wilson increasingly saw German policy on central Europe as a danger to his Open Door Policy.[37]

In light of the ostentatious display of global power by the German empire under Wilhelm II, this is not surprising. If one summarizes and contrasts the overall geopolitical visions of the two states, as the American political scientist and historian David Calleo has done, it becomes clear that Germany and the United States "were on a collision course at the beginning of the century that was dictated by their differing views of the future world order and the place they hoped to occupy in it. . . . America's geopolitical dreams centered on a Pax Americana designed to supplant the Pax Britannica, which was doomed to disappear. Wilson's program during the First World War lent concrete shape to these dreams. The United States pursued the goal of reviving and perfecting its own version of a liberal world order that had evolved in the middle of the nineteenth century. Its guiding principles were to be free trade capitalism, national self-determination, liberal democracy, and a world parliament. Wilson's program formed the outline of what the United States was to implement after the Second World War with far greater resolve. In the final analysis it implied American global hegemony."[38]

In contrast, the future envisioned by the Germany of Wilhelm II involved the acquisition of the status of a world power that was bound to destroy the European balance of power, which Germany saw as being fundamentally nothing more than the ideology of its global political rivals.

The contradictory nature of these geopolitical visions was to a certain extent mirrored in the contradictory nature of the methods employed, and above all of the internal orders. The American concept of peaceful change, which was nurtured by democratic traditions and the awareness of the factual growing strength of the United States, was regarded with more than a little distrust by Germany. This became evident in connection with the American policy of arbitration, even if, like Pommerin, one believes that the differences between the geostrategic situation of the two countries constitute the main reason for the divergent nature of German policy.[39]

With regard to the contradictory nature of the internal orders, Americans tended to emphasize "the differences in the form of government, the civil liberties enjoyed by American citizens, who were not required to do military service, were not subject to other kinds of coercion by the state, to state control, or indeed at the mercy of the authoritarian character of class-based domination in Germany." Germans, on the other hand, pointed to "vulgarly democratic, 'disorderly' and plutocratic features of American social life or to such dangerous similarities as the blockade of the Confederate states in the Civil War and a future blockade of the German coasts." The distance to Germany meant that the cultural and social predilections of the American upper class, which had always favored London and Paris, were able to acquire a political dimension, especially as imperialist competition with the powers of the entente, Britain and France, was on the wane. Thus "similarities and areas of common ground were both sought and discovered, for example, the Anglo-Saxon heritage, Protestant nonconformism, republican government, and also a certain middle-class stability that was so badly lacking in the absolutism of Wilhelm II. Middle-class America, however strongly it may have been armed or indeed was arming itself, considered the ostentatious display of power by Wilhelmine Germany to be an indecent demonstration of might that disqualified it from the start for an imperialist 'partnership,' even one of a passing kind."[40]

The German declaration of unrestricted submarine warfare gave the final impetus to America to enter the war on the side of the western powers. But the real reasons—and in this context it has been possible only to allude to them—went deeper and were far more complex. Their political meaning in terms of realpolitik was clearly recognized by certain American politicians and diplomats, whose number and importance in the United States should not be overestimated—although it should not be underestimated, either. Even before the outbreak of the war they had argued that a German victory in some kind of European war would pose a threat to the political and economic interests of the United States for it could lead to the predominance of a European state both on land and at sea. An undefeated Britain was believed to constitute the most important guarantee for the stability and preservation of the European balance of power, and only in this way was it possible to guarantee that the economic development of the United States would not be encumbered by an extensive arms buildup. For this reason America, even if it were to observe strict neutrality at the beginning, would feel compelled in the case of an impending British defeat to become actively involved in a European war—on the side of Britain.[41] A year after the outbreak of the war it became clear to President Wilson that "in case Europe falls under the domination of a single militarist group, peace and democracy for our country are going to be in grave danger, I shall have to urge American intervention."[42] Of course, it was not his intention to strengthen the British empire. The opposite was the case. Whereas a German victory would endanger the Monroe Doctrine, an Allied victory "without the assistance of the United States" would encourage the British to attempt "to dominate the commercial world."[43]

Thus in 1917 the transatlantic war coalition materialized as a common response to a threat that affected both Europe and America, although in different ways. There was also disagreement regarding what should happen in the event of peace. From an American point of view, victory was not supposed to replace the predominance of Germany with that of another European great power. Rather, the United States favored a peaceful order that would give it the best possible opportunity to develop and prosper.

4. INVOLVEMENT WITH OR CONTAINMENT OF SOVIET RUSSIA

In the very year that the United States entered the war under the motto "The world must be made safe for democracy," a new dimension was given to the transatlantic debate on a new peaceful order by the success of the October Revolution, which saw itself as the start of world revolution. This created a new situation, one that contained the tendency toward bipolarization.

The diametrically opposed ideas of international socialism and communism and its liberal and democratic counterpart now found their most direct expression in Lenin's Bolshevik Russia and in Wilson's liberal capitalist and democratic America. Thus in prototype form the bipolar nature of the East-West conflict was already a reality.[44] However, the division of power in the international system was still multipolar and had not yet become bipolar. Thus the fate of the European system of states was of decisive importance. Lenin knew full well that the future of world revolution would be decided in the highly industrialized states of western Europe. Wilson also looked to Europe, hoping to find with its democracies the "community of ideals and of interests" that was to form the core of the new peaceful order. In fact Wilson's policy was directed not only against Lenin's revolutionary "anti-imperialism," but also against the "traditional imperialism" of the west European great powers and of the German empire.

It was the "vision of a global order beyond power politics" that was to be characterized by free world trade, by cooperation between states on the basis of international law, by democratic kinds of government and society, and by international and capitalist trade relations (for example, the Open Door Policy).[45]

To be convincing, liberal and democratic policies had to be distinct from reactionary tendencies, both internally and internationally. Thus Wilson only reluctantly allowed the United States to participate in the military intervention of France, Britain, and Japan in the Russian civil war. Initially this seemed justified in the context of the "old" conflict—that is, to reestablish the eastern front and, after the bilateral German-Soviet peace of Brest-Litovsk, to prevent the formation of a Russo-German bloc, and to restrain the unilateral expansion of the Japanese sphere of influence. However, military intervention increasingly became an anti-Bolshevik affair, giving succor to the counterrevolutionary forces during the civil war.[46]

Yet after Germany had been defeated, the policy of intervention did not turn into determined military action by the Allied and associated powers. The French idea of a large-scale anti-Bolshevik crusade came to nothing as a result of opposition from Britain and above all from the United States, as did the attempts by vanquished Germany to come to an arrangement with the victorious powers by forming a common anti-Bolshevik front. But it is noteworthy that as early as the Versailles Conference the question of how communism could be contained or, considering the Bolshevik Revolution in Russia, how the reorganization of the international system could be achieved played a significant (though admittedly not a predominant) role.[47]

The United States (and Britain) hoped for change within Russia in order to integrate a democratic and noncommunist Russia into the western community of states.[48] Instead of military force, the American government preferred to use economic means of influencing Russia and to contain the Bolshevik Revolution in central and eastern Europe. To this end the food aid program that Herbert Hoover, who later became U.S. secretary of trade and then U.S. president, organized for the liberated countries was initially designed to include Russia, although eventually it was implemented only in the central and east European states and in Germany.

President Wilson described Hoover's "American Relief Administration" as "the second American expeditionary force to save Europe."[49] It was in fact a kind of "proto–Marshall Plan" designed to stabilize Europe.[50]

In light of the Bolshevik threat and the danger of a communist seizure of power in central Europe, the reintegration of a democratic, liberal, and capitalist Germany into the western community of states, which was the aim of American policy in the First World War from the very beginning, acquired the additional significance of being an element in the anti-Bolshevik policy of containment. The overriding importance of social stabilization against revolutionary tendencies meant that in November 1918 President Wilson would even have been prepared to accept the establishment of a constitutional monarchy in response to his demands for the removal of the autocratic regime in Germany. As Secretary of State Robert Lansing wrote in a confidential letter on October 12, 1918, "We must not allow it [Bolshevism] to become the master of the peoples of central Europe. There it would become an even greater danger for the rest of the world than Prussianism."[51]

The nightmare of a Russo-German concentration of power even led some of the American presidential advisers, in direct contrast to previous policy, to recommend a rapprochement with the Bolshevik regime. Thus, on March 26, 1919, presidential adviser Colonel Edward Mandell House noted in his diary, "If we did not make terms with them [the Soviet regime] it was certain that as soon as we made peace with Germany, Russia and Germany would link together, thereby realizing my prophecy that, sooner or later, everything east of the Rhine would be arranged against the western powers."[52] However, President Wilson rejected this policy approach, and adhered strictly to his refusal to negotiate with the Soviets or to recognize their regime.

After the failure of the policy of intervention, the west European states and the United States pursued a policy of isolating Bolshevik Russia. The erection of a *cordon sanitaire* of central and east European states was to prevent the Bolshevik Revolution from spreading to western Europe, and at the same time make it more difficult for Bolshevik Russia and vanquished Germany to form a united front. This goal was, of course, shared by the United States: "A strong Poland is the greatest importance to the peace of the world and is a bulwark against Russia and also against Germany."[53] Even after Germany had become a democracy, in terms of power politics the issue from a European and American point of view was one of dual containment: of Soviet Russia and Germany. The policy of diplomatic nonrecognition and isolation of the Bolshevik regime was designed to keep alive the possibility of a later reintegration of a democratic Russia and at the same time to make this path attractive for opposition forces within Russia. However, the European states soon gave up the policy of isolation and cooperated in a pragmatic manner with the Soviet regime, partly for economic and partly for political reasons.

Britain was the first of the victorious west European states to make a move in this direction. Prime Minister David Lloyd George believed that the United Kingdom could not do without the Russian market, and thus the bilateral contacts that first dealt with the repatriation of prisoners of war (in 1920) led to de facto recognition and to a trade agreement in 1921.[54]

Internally the Weimar Republic was faced with the problem of how to deal with the revolutionary activities of the Communist Party of Germany, which were supported and steered from Moscow via the Comintern. Thus in terms of domestic policy the government of the German Reich clearly pursued a policy of containment. But both economic factors (the traditional interest in the Russian market and the current need to increase the level of exports) and the German government's main political goal, the revision of the Treaty of Versailles, spoke in favor of coming to some kind of foreign policy arrangement with Soviet Russia.[55]

The fact that Germany for its part wished to use Russia to "balance" its overall revisionist policy and as a "backing" for its policy toward the west, and that Soviet Russia for its part wished to prevent the formation of a united western front that included Germany and also needed a favorably inclined Germany as a shield against the western powers, was of crucial importance for the creation of a German-Soviet special relationship. These coinciding political interests led, as the German historian Klaus Hildebrand has argued, to the temporarily identical goal of "creating a joint counterpoise to the entente in the context of European balance-of-power politics, thus gaining political room for maneuver."[56]

With the 1922 Treaty of Rapallo, Germany, which feared that the western powers and Soviet Russia might otherwise reach an agreement at its expense, officially broke out of the united western front. It reestablished diplomatic relations with Soviet Russia and renounced claims resulting from the country's policies of nationalization. The two governments accorded each other most-favored-nation status and agreed to continue the policy of economic concessions that had been initiated before.[57]

The Treaty of Rapallo (which, it was believed, included further secret accords) suddenly raised old fears in western Europe and the United States that "a union of purpose between Germany and Russia" might materialize, that a German-Soviet bloc was emerging, and that this might endanger integration of both states into the west.[58]

Soon after Rapallo the other west European states also officially abandoned the policy of isolation, and 1924 became the "year of recognition," in which Britain, Italy, Norway, Austria, Greece, Sweden, Denmark, China, and France established diplomatic ties with Soviet Russia. Despite some vacillation, which was largely the result of revolutionary Comintern activities, the west European countries now began to pursue a pragmatic and cooperative policy toward Russia.

However, the United States officially continued to adhere to the policy of isolation until 1933. Thus American policy toward Russia differed significantly from the variants of a more integrative and cooperative policy toward Russia adopted by European countries. In particular, the U.S. government rejected the policy pursued by the west European states of setting up an international consortium for the economic exploitation of the Russian market. Such a policy ran counter to the principle of the Open Door Policy, and thus from an American point of view there was a danger that "substantial investments by America in any consortium will fall under British control and management."[59] The United States was clearly unwilling to finance British predominance on the Russian market with its own money. Nor did it wish to encourage German predominance.

Secretary of Trade Hoover staked a U.S. claim to "the leadership in the reconstruction of Russia when the proper moment arrives."[60] This implied a wait-and-see attitude until the situation in Russia permitted capitalist involvement. Then, he hoped, the affinity between the Russian and the American peoples and the sympathy that in his opinion would be the result of American aid to Russia might benefit American industry—without the mediation and participation of Germany. Until such time, the policy of isolation continued.

Yet there was also a more integrative and cooperative tendency within the American government. The more improbable the prospect of an early collapse of the Bolshevik regime became, and the greater the competition among the west Europeans for preferential trading rights in the Soviet Union, the more some American officials began to consider economic cooperation below the level of recognition. They justified a policy of this kind with an argument that in a variety of guises has subsequently resurfaced in every period of détente: "In all probability it will be easier to hasten its transformation into a more or less normal representative government, having a more or less normal economic policy, by beginning to do business with it rather than by holding off."[61] However, Secretary of State Hughes and his successor, Frank B. Kellogg, continued to pursue a policy of isolation, and asked the west European states to work together.

Yet a united western front did not materialize. Furthermore, the economic *cordon sanitaire* had long been broken, even by American industry, and on several occasions American exports to Russia even surpassed those of the leading nation in this respect, Germany.[62] At the end of the 1920s the number of cooperation agreements that American industrial corporations concluded with Soviet Russia increased dramatically. In the interests of its own economy the American government tolerated these activities, although they strengthened that of the Soviet Union, thus contributing indirectly to the failure of isolationism.

In the final analysis, however, it was not the attractive nature of the Russian market that led to a reorientation of American policy on Russia. The nationalist and expansionist policies pursued by Japan and Germany and the reaction of the Soviet Union (and its policy of collective security) were the real reasons why the United States shifted to a policy of incorporating Russia into global politics without there having been a change in its political and economic system. "The idea was forming in the minds of both Roosevelt and Hull that Japan and Germany might be sobered if the breach between the United States and the Soviet Union were healed."[63]

In 1933, with this goal in mind, the American policy of isolation was replaced by a policy of partial cooperation. In this way, U.S. policy toward Russia was brought into line with that of the west Europeans—under the shadow of the common threat posed by the imperialist intentions of Germany and Japan. The need to form a counterpoise—after the interlude of the Hitler-Stalin pact—made it necessary for the opponents in the East-West conflict to pursue "antagonistic cooperation."

5. THE PATTERN OF TRANSATLANTIC RELATIONS IN THE 1920s

Germany constituted the main problem in the reshaping of transatlantic relations as long as, in the 1920s, the global ambitions of Soviet Russia were held in check by the construction of "socialism in one country." In view of the new balance of power, it became clear that the solution to the problem would depend on the kind of role that the United States, the "dominant world economic power," wished to play in the transatlantic relationship or in fact already played.[64]

During and at the end of the war President Wilson was firmly convinced that American power would suffice to implement his new world order once it came to a peace treaty.[65] In London, where he stopped off on his way to Paris, he declared: "They [the American soldiers] fought to do away with an old order and to establish a new one, and the center and characteristic of the old order was that unstable thing which we used to call the 'balance of power'—a thing in which the balance was determined by the sword. . . . [T]hat sort of thing should end now and forever."[66]

However, Wilson and his advisers were well aware that even in the new world order, the balance of power was of crucial importance. From

Paris the president issued important orders to increase American power and to balance that of Britain.[67] However, it was a question not of military, but of economic might, and thus a new liberal world order would permit the preeminent power of the United States to become fully evident—in the typical conjunction of American business and government (the "cooperative state").[68] The rejection of European balance-of-power politics was based on U.S. hopes of achieving economic hegemony.[69]

This concept was also the reason why the American government was strictly against allowing American resources to continue to flow through Allied channels after the end of the war, and why it rejected the continuation of institutionalized wartime cooperation. The directive was that "this government will not agree to any program that even looks like inter-Allied control of our economic resources after peace."[70] Thus the United States terminated its participation in the various inter-Allied councils and at the Conference of Paris opposed the idea of retaining the Supreme Economic Council as an agency for inter-Allied economic planning.[71]

Striving for an independent use of power was in line with Wilson's original concept, which was to act as a mediator at the peace conference on the basis of the Fourteen Points. However, two important preconditions had already disappeared when the Versailles Conference began. "The one was that the German adversary should retain a certain amount of power and political clout. This had been removed by the armistice. The Allies now possessed precisely the kind of 'surfeit' of 'security' about which Wilson had warned. America could no longer bring about peace as a de facto independent mediator between two parties, but was forced to approach the defeated adversary as a victor together with the other victors. The second precondition for the success of the American strategy of peace was the unchallenged position of the American president in his own country. After the American mid-term elections this was no longer the case."[72] Thus the agreements negotiated at Versailles combined elements of collective security and the balance of power.

France abandoned its attempts to guarantee its security against defeated Germany by annexing territory west of the Rhine because Britain and the United States held out the prospect of (and finally concluded) treaties with France that guaranteed France's territorial integrity against an unprovoked attack. Wilson believed that the Franco-American treaty could be combined with the League of Nations, which was designed to provide an international framework for global political cooperation.[73] Yet it was precisely this link between the League of Nations and the Franco-American guarantee treaty that led to the League's rejection by the U.S. Senate. Senator Henry Cabot Lodge, Senate Republican leader and chairman of the Foreign Relations Committee, and many other opponents of the League of Nations were in favor of a continuation of the wartime alliance. On the other hand, the collective assistance stipulated in the charter of the League of Nations was seen to violate the Monroe Doctrine and thus American freedom of action. It would enable European powers to interfere in the Western Hemisphere and contained an unlimited U.S. commitment to intervene, which in the future would have excluded the participation of the U.S. Senate in this central decision-making area. For this reason (although the Monroe Doctrine had been expressly recognized in the charter of the League of Nations), membership in the League of Nations was rejected by the Republican opposition, whereas French security guarantees were welcomed.

However, the majority of senators opposed to Wilson's plan in its entirety certainly agreed that a recurrence of a threat in Europe would lead to renewed transatlantic action. Thus directly after the end of the war Senator Philander Knox, the former secretary of state, had formulated the "New American Doctrine": "If a situation should arise in which any power or combination of powers should, directly or indirectly, menace the freedom and peace of Europe, the United States would regard such a situation with grave concern as a menace to its freedom and peace and would consult with other powers affected with a view to concerted action for the removal of such menace."[74] This was the line of continuity that linked the American decision to enter into the transatlantic war coalition with the policy of the new Republican administration (which continued to be of importance thereafter). The American policy of stabilization in Europe at the beginning of the 1920s, which Secretary of State Hughes outlined with the words "independence and cooperation," was a policy of mediation and balance, exerted by a "mighty world power" cooperating without institutional constraints.[75]

From an American point of view the danger of destabilization in Europe now emanated not from a weakened Germany (with which the United States concluded a separate peace treaty in 1921), but from one of the victorious powers, France. Yet the fact that the American guarantee treaty had failed to materialize enhanced France's attempts to revise the Treaty of Versailles to ensure French hegemony utilizing the means that the treaty placed at its disposal: the military occupation of the Rhineland and the German obligation to pay reparations, where noncompliance made it possible to apply sanctions.[76] This strategy was designed to bring about an economic or political separation of the occupied areas from Germany, and to establish a link between the economic potential of the Ruhr and the French economy under overall French control. The idea of Franco-German economic links was also considered in western Germany, although here it was hoped that the economic predominance of German industry would be the decisive factor.

The American government replied to the "European" idea of economic links under German or French control with its own "Atlantic" concept. An international commission of experts with American participation ("a supreme court of business judgment") was to investigate the situation in Germany in order to ascertain German economic strength, and to suggest the regulation of reparations in an economically reasonable manner, with the help of an international loan (to be placed primarily on the American market). And for a time the American government was even prepared to make concessions with regard to the regulation of inter-Allied debts—that is, with regard to the question that, more than any other, was of decisive importance for the economic and financial balance of power between the west European states and the United States, and that adversely affected transatlantic relations throughout the interwar period.[77]

After the diplomatic efforts of the United States had failed, partly because of France, but also because of Britain, Secretary of State Hughes went on the offensive with his famous speech in New Haven on December 29, 1922. His goal was to create a reference point for the subsequent resumption of American mediation with his plan for a commission of experts—for the time, that is, when (as he anticipated) the impending occupation of the Ruhr would emerge as a political failure with both sides experiencing their "bit of chaos."

The American government used the temporary cessation of its mediation efforts, which was forced on it by the occupation of the Ruhr on January 11, 1923, to strengthen its position bilaterally with both Britain and France:

— On February 3 the American government concluded the debt agreement with Britain on far more favorable terms than had originally been stipulated by Congress. This removed an important obstacle to Anglo-American cooperation with regard to the regulation of reparations.

— In July and August 1923 France finally ratified the Treaty of Washington on naval disarmament and the Four Power Naval Treaty, which constituted the centerpiece of American security policy and arms control in the Pacific. It was the need to take into consideration this previously unresolved question that had made it seem expedient to Hughes not to proceed too vigorously with his admonishments to France regarding the question of reparations. Such reticence was now no longer necessary.

— The American government took advantage of Germany's position of weakness in order, in a model trade agreement, to introduce the new American trade policy, which was based on the principle of nondiscrimination and unqualified reciprocal most-favored-nation status, and to enforce it throughout Europe. The draft agreement was submitted for consideration in July 1923, marking the start of the implementation of the new policy. In the final analysis, the treaty documented the determination of the United States to preserve Germany as an independent nation with equal rights, and to integrate it into a liberal international order in which there would be no economic blocs.[78]

News of the separate negotiations between the Ruhr industrialists and the chemical industry with the French and Belgian occupation forces demonstrably strengthened the American resolve to become involved, and thus had an additional catalytic effect. These developments were wholly against American interests. If such economic cooperation came about, Hughes feared, a great industrial power would arise that would have to seek new markets for its products and prove to be a powerful competitor for the United States on the world market. It was in the interests of America to end the French occupation of the Ruhr, to prevent the threat of a west European concentration of power that might be the result of the occupation, and to consolidate the European market by regulating the issue of reparations. This broad social and political consensus, which was clearly articulated in the United States in the summer and autumn of 1923, formed the basis of what proved to be successful attempts at U.S. mediation, leading to the appointment of a committee of experts, the so-called Dawes Committee.

The Dawes Plan, which the committee subsequently devised, was adopted at the London Conference in the summer of 1924 (attended by U.S. Ambassador Kellogg and American bankers) and marked the "end of French predominance in Europe."[79] It prevented both the creation of a center of west European economic power and the diversion of American economic resources through British channels or under British control. Instead, it established an economic balance of power in Europe that was controlled and "held" by the United States to some extent in conjunction with Britain. To put it another way, the Ruhr conflict was followed by an American "economic peace" that preserved Germany as an independent counterpoise to France, and in which the United States was the informal "balancer." (In terms of security policy Britain assumed a balancer function on account of the Locarno Treaty, which President Coolidge rightly described as "the result of the Dawes Report.")

Thus, America pacified Europe with American capital and with American"financial advisers"—that is, by means of a transnational policy.[80] It established a Pax Americana, which made possible the economic and political stabilization of Germany and Europe, although, as was soon to become apparent, only for a short time.

The continual flow of capital to Europe, and especially to Germany, was also designed to overcome a contradiction that placed a considerable strain on transatlantic relations in the 1920s (and beyond). With the Fordney-McCumber Tariff of 1922 the largest creditor nation closed off its internal market to European competition, thus making it impossible for the Europeans to earn the dollars that they needed to repay their debts and to pay reparations.

The American government argued that it was right to say that in the final analysis international debt would have to be paid for by increasing exports. However, by means of dollar loans, private debt would take the place of international governmental debt, and private debt could always be extended by negotiation until a favorable opportunity for repayment arose. Thus America could lend $625 million annually to private German borrowers over a period of 20 years until it had reached a position as a creditor nation that resembled that of Britain before the war. Therefore a reduction in American tariffs was unnecessary to enable Europeans to pay reparations or to repay debts.[81]

Thus American policy in Europe was consciously aimed at establishing American economic predominance. However, it was not restricted to economic affairs. In terms of security policy the economic peace was to be underpinned by arms control and disarmament (as had been attempted for the Pacific area at the Washington Conference in 1922). This was rejected above all by France and Britain. France wished to maintain its military predominance over Germany, which had been forced by the Treaty of Versailles to engage in unilateral disarmament and to accept severe armaments restrictions; Britain believed that its naval power was in danger. On the other hand, Germany supported American policy on disarmament in order to achieve armaments parity—a strategy that in fact turned out to be a success in 1932. Thus Germany adroitly used U.S. material involvement to achieve a stepwise revision of the terms of the Treaty of Versailles by adapting the American concept of "peaceful change."

France, in the period of relative stability, once more tried to return to the abortive guarantee agreement of 1919, and attempted to tie the United States into a policy of collective security that was based on the status quo. This was the point of French Foreign Minister Aristide Briand's proposal in April 1927: in a bilateral agreement the United States and France should renounce war between the two countries forever and declare it to be illegal. However, the American government undermined this initiative by suggesting a multilateral treaty designed to outlaw war in place of a bilateral pact. Thus the Kellogg-Briand Pact of 1928 did not institute a special Franco-American relationship. Instead of falling in line with France's status-quo policy, the American government pursued a universalist policy of peaceful change, and this came a long way toward satisfying German revisionist demands.

When, in the negotiations leading up to the pact that was designed to outlaw war, it became obvious that the United States could not be persuaded to agree to the French security policy, the French government switched to a European strategy. It now attempted to organize a European counterpoise to the United States and tried to obtain support for "the expedience of uniting Europe against American supremacy."[82]

Two years later, the French foreign minister picked up, on an official level, ideas that had been propagated by various private organizations (including the Pan European Union, of which he was honorary president). Briand now proposed the "organization of a European Federal Union" that preserved the principle of the individual state's sovereignty. All European countries that were members of the League of Nations (and therefore not the Soviet Union) were to enter into a "federal relationship," with a permanent governmental council, a permanent political affairs committee, and a secretariat. In practical and procedural terms, economic cooperation (the aim being to establish a common market) was to be subordinated to the regulation of political problems. However, because of the proposed precedence of the problem of security, the German and British governments interpreted this proposal as a French attempt "definitely to secure the existing state of affairs and thus existing borders" (including Germany's eastern borders, the revision of which Germany insisted on) by means of a new European organization.[83] The German Foreign Ministry commented: "This status quo is to be ensured by a smaller circle than the League of Nations, because in such a smaller circle the influence of France would be even greater. And at the same time our non-European relations [America and Russia] are to be curtailed."[84]

It is hardly surprising that Briand's proposal came to nothing. There were numerous objections to it in view of the irreconcilable difference between the French policy of the status quo and German revisionist demands. Furthermore, the formation of a common European counterpoise to the Soviet Union *and* to the United States (and this, despite assurances to the contrary, would have been the foreign policy effect of a federalization) was in neither the economic nor the political interests of Germany. Foreign Minister Gustav Stresemann had already argued in connection with the negotiations for the Kellogg-Briand Pact that "in the future Germany will need American support in the field of foreign policy" and for this reason would not allow itself to be drawn into an "alliance against America."[85] Rather, the German government expressly greeted the preservation and strengthening of American "arbitration interests" in Europe, and avoided anything that might have been construed as the "exclusion" of the United States.[86]

In fact the United States feared that the nascent political and economic understanding and cooperation between the European states contained a potentially anti-American element. A slight suspicion of this kind had already surfaced after the conclusion of the Locarno Treaties. The ensuing negotiations between the French and German governments and the formation of continental cartels, which began to flourish at this time, only increased American concerns.[87] In the negotiations for the pact outlawing war, the United States used its excellent relations with Germany to prevent the formation of a united European front. And when Briand's European plan was finally made public, the United States encouraged the German government (partly through direct intervention by the American chargé d'affaires in Berlin) to block the anti-American intentions of the French from the very start.[88] Thus in the 1920s the concept of organizing European cooperation on federal lines met with opposition from the strongest economic power.

This demonstrates the fundamental contradiction that characterized American policy on Europe at this time. On the one hand, the United States, in its own interests, wished to secure political and economic stability in Europe and a compromise between the various nations; this was the precondition for its economic involvement. Thus it was even prepared to act as an arbitrator if required (as discussed earlier). On the other hand, it insisted on a separate and bilateral regulation of its relations with each European state, suspecting that joint European moves were motivated by anti-American tendencies, or ones that adversely affected American interests.

A way of overcoming this dilemma seemed possible through strategic partnerships with Germany and Britain. The United States urged the Weimar Republic to pursue a consistent policy of compromise with its European neighbors, but simultaneously encouraged it to prevent the formation of an anti-American European bloc in various areas. By means of large American loans and direct investments (the largest on the Continent), the Weimar Republic became the American bridgehead on the Continent, a strategic partner and a firm supporter of the United States. This relationship was wholly in the interests of Germany and paid rich dividends. Finally, in the economic crisis, President Hoover came to the aid of Germany with a moratorium on debt, because the United States, as a result of its great capital investment, was "tied up with Germany's situation." And when France refused to support the American policy of peaceful change in support of German revisionist demands, the American president saw "nothing in the future but a lineup between Germany, Britain, and ourselves against France."[89]

The American-German strategic partnership was thus linked to the American-British "special relationship," which in the 1920s had developed into an "informal entente" that was not entirely unproblematic.[90]

Competition between the British sterling and the U.S. dollar had been decided in favor of the latter as a result of the Dawes Plan. However, thereafter the close cooperation between the Federal Reserve Bank of New York and the Bank of England became the center of monetary management.[91] Simultaneously, in other policy areas (for example, disarmament and trade) there was a significant conflict of interests. In an internal Foreign Office analysis in November 1927, a war with the United States was even deemed "not unthinkable." And in the summer of the same year the possibility of an Anglo-American war was mentioned in a conversation between U.S. Secretary of Commerce Hoover and British Ambassador Esme Howard.[92] After the successful conclusion of the London naval conference in April 1930 on the basis of parity (although Britain was granted the right to have more cruisers), Britain—unlike the United States—made full use of its armaments quotas.[93]

In short, in the 1920s a transatlantic security community had not yet materialized. Rather, there was a "kaleidoscopically" changing community of purposes between the European great powers and America that varied from one problem to another.[94] Cooperation and competition existed side by side.

Significantly, transatlantic cooperation in the stabilization phase was closest in the area of monetary policy and with regard to loans. However, the most important American figure in this area, Governor Benjamin Strong of the Federal Reserve Bank of New York, rejected a formal institutionalization of this kind of cooperation on the lines of a conference, partly using the revealing argument that the Federal Reserve Bank would form the only bond market, whereas all the other representatives would be debtors, and thus overrule America on all important decisions. "He would have to be sure of having one more vote than all the borrowers combined."[95]

Despite such reservations, which were wholly in keeping with the official maxim of "independence and cooperation," under Strong's successors there emerged a certain institutionalization of transatlantic cooperation among the central banks in the shape of the Bank for International Settlements. This was established as part of the Young Plan (1929–30) and was under American control, although without the formal membership of the Federal Reserve System (which affected its value in terms of cooperation from the very start). The functions that were to be given to the BIS went far beyond the task of dealing with reparations (the "depoliticization" and "commercialization" of reparations payments). Owen D. Young, chairman of the General Electric Company and head of the second export committee on reparations in 1929, hoped that if the BIS concentrated the whole of the world's loan structure in one place, the Kellogg-Briand Pact would become "practically effective . . . because nothing except peace could exist."[96] Economic integration, which in the stabilization phase had progressed under the leadership of large American companies in both transatlantic and global terms, was the real backdrop for American hopes that "economic peace" would lead to "political peace." "We shall never have . . . political integration until we have first economic integration . . . economics must lead . . . and politics must follow."[97]

6. THE ORIGINS OF THE SECOND TRANSATLANTIC WAR COALITION

As a result of the world economic crisis—which led to a cessation of the flow of American capital to Europe and to the Great Depression, which affected all industrialized countries—the process of integration came to a standstill and then gave way to disintegration. In Europe this led to the collapse of the American "economic peace." At the same time, the Pacific order that had been established at the Washington Conference collapsed as a result of Japan's aggressive policy of expansion.[98] The joint transatlantic policy of stabilization pursued under informal American leadership and with American capital was now superseded by national and regional policies of stabilization, a development that not even the World Economic Conference held in London in the summer of 1933 was able to arrest, especially since the strongest economic power, the United States, now acted unilaterally and abandoned the gold standard. In place of the "gold standard" dollar of the 1920s, which had functioned because of cooperation between the new and old centers of monetary control (New York and London), there now arose rival regional economic blocs centered on the dollar, sterling, gold, the yen, and the mark, coupled with the regionalization of trade policy.[99]

The new Democratic government in Washington veered between a national and an international approach, although initially it concentrated on the domestic reforms that were part of the New Deal. And as late as March 1935, President Franklin Roosevelt asked the State Department to investigate whether, in view of the futility of a global policy of stabilization, the regional approach (dividing the world into "self-contained economic units") might be a feasible alternative.[100]

Yet the realization that the United States was dependent on the world economy and the growing challenge of the National Socialism movement caused Roosevelt to shift to the universalist policy that Secretary of State Cordell Hull had advocated from the start, and that he had initiated with the Trade Agreements Act in June 1934. Its aim was to restore a multilateral system of free trade based on most-favored-nation status. This was wholly in line with the Open Door Policy.

In contrast to the situation that had occurred at the beginning of the 1920s, such a policy could no longer be implemented with the new German regime. In fact, the opposite was the case, for in October 1934 the Third Reich withdrew from the 1923 trade agreement (Secretary of State Hull considered this an act of aggression against the whole American system of trade treaties). In the 1930s, in the phase "between revision and expansion,"[101] National Socialist Germany created a large central European sphere of influence, moved increasingly into the Latin American market, and collided with American interests in both the former and the latter.[102]

Hull initially continued to hope for the reintegration of Germany in the area of trade policy. However, in the monetary sphere the U.S. policy of international cooperation, which succeeded the nationalist phase, was designed from the very start to be a transatlantic counterpoise to National Socialist Germany and Fascist Italy.

In 1934, after the stabilization of the dollar, the Stabilization Fund was established. This made it possible to extend loans to foreign governments. A year later a coordinated policy was in principle agreed to by the United States, Britain, and France and later finalized in the Tripartite Agreement of September 25, 1936. On this occasion transatlantic cooperation was not, as in the 1920s, the work of private bankers or the governor of the Federal Reserve Bank. The government itself, which was represented by Secretary of the Treasury Henry Morgenthau and his aides, now assumed direct responsibility. With regard to the forms and methods employed, American foreign policy, under the pressure of events in Europe, began to act in terms of the "regulatory state."[103] Later, at the end of the war, this developed into the International Monetary Fund (IMF) and other institutions of international cooperation.[104]

Finally, the clearest sign of the formation of a transatlantic counterpoise against Nazi Germany was the Anglo-American trade agreement of

November 17, 1938, and this is how it was perceived in Germany ("a symbol of Anglo-American cooperation in all areas").[105]

Yet it would be wrong simply to attribute this polarization to the expansion of German power and the formation of a transatlantic counterweight. Polarization between the western democracies and the National Socialist dictatorship and its ideology of race was a decisive factor from the very beginning only in the area of ideology and with regard to concepts of order, where it continued to be one. In political and diplomatic terms the United States toyed with the idea of establishing "working relations" with the Third Reich, and there were attempts to reintegrate Nazi Germany in the context of a global compromise (a policy that was especially advocated by Undersecretary of State Sumner Welles). Furthermore, there were the all-too-familiar British attempts at appeasement (from the Naval Treaty of 1935 to the Munich Agreement of 1938).[106] Even after the Anglo-American trade treaty, reservations about cooperation with the United States and the idea of a European economic bloc directed against the United States that included Germany continued to play a significant role in official British policy—until the beginning of the war.[107] Only after Hitler had defeated Britain's European allies did the alternative that had been suggested in 1938, and that had remained on the agenda, begin to determine the overall policy direction. That alternative was marked by the Lend-Lease Agreement and the Atlantic Charter.

The formation of the Anglo-American coalition shattered Hitler's hopes of forcing Britain to support him, although it confirmed his belief that apart from the Soviet Union—which, after its temporary neutralization by means of the Hitler-Stalin pact in August 1939, he now intended to subjugate—the United States was the real opponent of his policy of hegemony and global dominion. However, his gamble that the nation that was "clearly the principal opponent in the distant future" would remain on the sidelines long enough to enable him to consolidate German power on the Continent proved to be an illusion. Paradoxically, the alliance with Japan, which was designed to distract U.S. attention from Europe and weaken Britain, led to direct U.S. military involvement in the war coalition (which until then had been possible only in informal terms, partly because of the constraints that the American Congress had placed on the president through its neutrality legislation, had been possible only in informal terms).[108]

The German attack on the Soviet Union and Germany's declaration of war on the United States (which followed the Japanese onslaught) led to a grouping that combined the antagonistic cooperation between the opponents of the East-West conflict with the transatlantic alliance—as a result of the common threat posed by the Axis powers and their striving for supremacy. As in the First World War, transatlantic cooperation materialized as a result of the impending defeat of Britain, and this finally led to the formation of the counterweight. Prior to this there had been consultations and the beginnings of joint action of the kind envisaged by the "New American Doctrine" to deal with possible threats to peace and freedom.

Thus in 1940 Britain had "to choose between Hitler's 'Pax Germanica' and Roosevelt's 'Pax Americana,'" and decided in favor of "junior partnership on the side of the Americans."[109] In view of the threat to its existence posed by German supremacy, it seemed preferable to accept American hegemony within the transatlantic relationship, especially since the common ideological opposition to the racism of National Socialism within the Anglo-Saxon community of values compensated for the political asymmetries. However, it was clear to an even greater extent than in the First World War that the decisive predominance of the United States in the transatlantic alliance would be crucial not only with regard to the conduct of the war, but also within the new peaceful order. As in the case of Wilson's Fourteen Points, the United States set out its universalist program in the Atlantic Charter. It called for the creation of a free internal order based on national self-determination, the establishment of a secure peace and of a liberal and nondiscriminatory world trade system (which was designed to ensure "access, on equal terms, to the trade and to the raw materials of the world" and "the fullest collaboration between all nations in the economic field"). That this was incompatible with both the restoration of the British empire and the traditional system of European states was obvious, not to mention the contrast between the American concept and that of a communist world order.

7. THE BEGINNINGS OF A NEW ORDER

The situation at the end of the war resembled that of 1918–19 inasmuch as Germany was once again defeated and the United States emerged as the true victor. Once again the differences between the victorious powers rendered the establishment of a stable peaceful order problematic. Furthermore, the concepts with regard to policy on Germany varied greatly, and there was a threat of economic chaos and of a socialist or communist takeover in Europe.

However, in addition to these similarities there were important quantitative and qualitative differences:

— Germany had not only been totally defeated, but was wholly at the mercy of the four victorious powers, who now jointly (although in separate zones of occupation) exercised complete authority over the country.

— In political terms Bolshevik Russia had turned into an expansionist great power, the Soviet Union. This meant that the spread of the Bolshevik Revolution with the help of the Red Army became a real danger, and inter-Allied differences to some extent became intersystemic differences.

— The relative strength of the United States was greater than ever in economic and military terms (both with regard to conventional weapons and because of its nuclear monopoly), signifying the former European great powers increased dependence on the United States.

— On the other hand, because of the wartime development of armaments and transportation technology, the United States became directly dependent on events in Europe, not only in economic terms, but also with regard to security policy.

— In general terms the nuclear weapons of mass destruction cast war as a means of settling international conflicts in a new and self-destructive light. The features that were reminiscent of 1918–19 and those that were new once again created a situation in which Germany became a major problem for American policy on Europe. This was part of a global concept and (compared with the interwar concept) was remarkably consistent in its direction. In other words, the policy designed by the Roosevelt-Hull administration and subsequently adopted by Truman took its bearings from the goal of a liberal world trade and economic order that was to be organized on the principles of multilateralism and nondiscrimination, and thus provided the United States with the best possible opportunity to increase its prosperity and secure a leading role. When compared with the similar concept of the Republican administration in the 1920s, this policy, the main aspects of which remained unchanged, had an important additional feature that took its bearings from the approach adopted by Wilson. In light of the failure of informal cooperation during the world economic crisis, the United States now decided to institutionalize multilateralism in the area of trade policy, and to ensure economic cooperation through institutionalized political cooperation. In real political terms this meant that the Bretton Woods monetary system and the envisaged international trade organization were complemented by the U.N. system. This arrangement (in contrast to the disagreement concerning the League of Nations) was approved by both parties. The ties that institutionalized cooperation of this kind could be reconciled with the traditional striving for independence (unilateralism) inasmuch as American predominance would provide the United States with a "natural" leadership advantage. Veto rights in the Security Council provided protection against being overruled by the majority. The belief that the Soviet Union would also be willing to become involved rested on the assumption that it would continue to pursue its advantageous economic cooperation with the United States because this was in its own interest. (Soviet participation in Bretton Woods and Dumbarton Oaks, and the Soviet application for a loan were taken as signs of this).[110]

It was thought that Britain and France would be willing to cooperate on account of their economic dependence on the United States, and this suggested that it would also be possible to implement the American concept of order and its particular goals (such as the abolition of the British preferential system and the dismantling of British and French colonialism).

In this American universalist concept there was no place for special transatlantic relationships—with the important exception of the bilateral cooperation between the United States and Britain in the nuclear sector (which went hand in hand with the "policy of exclusion" toward the Soviet Union) and bilateral temporary aid for Britain and France.[111] In other respects the West European "great powers," like all the states of the United Nations, were to be integrated into the new multilateral political, economic, and monetary institutions (IMF, World Trade Organization) and, as permanent members of the U.N. Security Council, would have a privileged position in the context of multilateral cooperation with the United States (and China and Russia). In other words, there was to be no such thing as a transatlantic special relationship. It was to be replaced by participation in the collective hegemony of the four (or five) "world policemen" within the framework of the United Nations.

However, the universalist concept of the United States was not only endangered by the Soviet Union with its policy of zones of influence in Central and Eastern Europe. During the war and in the buildup to the Potsdam Conference, Britain favored an alternative concept of order that was designed to provide support for the Commonwealth in a regionalist manner, and that, after it became clear that there would be a Soviet zone of influence in Central and Eastern Europe, sought to establish a counterweight in the shape of a West European bloc. That this alternative regionalist concept, in view of the balance of power in Europe, would in the end lead to the involvement of the United States, and to the formation of a transatlantic counterpoise, was clearly understood in American government circles, and initially rejected: "Since there is no longer power to balance in Europe, Britain would logically turn to the United States as the greatest potential source of support in developing an adequate counterpoise to Russia. Without the assured support of the United States, any combination of powers which Britain might be able to assemble would still leave Russia preponderantly strong."[112]

In the summer of 1945 the United States still gave priority to its universalist concept of cooperation. The frame of reference was "Europe *as a whole*." Of course, it was not in American interests to deny the United Kingdom protection against a possible threat from the Soviet Union. But at this juncture it was important to help to settle the Russo-British arguments in the interests of continuing cooperation among the great powers. "Until it is determined which course events in Europe will take—that is, whether Russia will collaborate or not—we should not take a positive stand one way or the other on this proposal to draw the nations of Western Europe into closer association."[113]

Whether this would be a success or a failure hinged on what happened in Germany. After plans for splitting the country up, which had been considered during the war, were discarded, the establishment of the four-power Control Council and then of the four-power Council of Foreign

Ministers represented the first attempts to institutionalize the universalist policy of order in Germany and Europe. "Such a council would tend to reduce the possibilities of unilateral action by either the Russians or the British and would serve as a useful interim means through which the United States could work for the liquidation of spheres of influence."[114]

Even more important was the American idea (which is frequently neglected in the literature) of concluding a four-power treaty on disarming Germany for a period of 25 years. Interestingly enough, this was suggested by the Republican opposition (Senator Arthur H. Vandenberg) and was taken up by Secretary of State James F. Byrnes.[115] Its general purpose was much the same, namely, "to weaken British and Soviet justifications for the maintenance of spheres of influence in Western and Eastern Europe respectively." At the same time (the analogy to the Franco-American guarantee treaty of 1919 is obvious) it was designed as a counterconcept to the French policy of fragmentation and territorial claims (that is, separating the Rhineland, the Ruhr, and the Saarland from the rest of Germany). The security problem with regard to Germany was to be solved in a four-power context—that is, together with the United States and the Soviet Union—and not by unilateral measures taken by the Soviet Union or France, by the formation of a West European bloc, or by means of bilateral treaties (such as the Franco-Soviet treaty or the Anglo-French treaty of Dunkerque). As had been the case after the First World War, the United States wished to preclude a concentration of power in Europe—whatever the grouping. The more it became apparent that the power resisting the implementation of American policy on Germany and pursuing a unilateralist policy was not or not only France, the more the proposed four-power treaty began to be directed against the possible threat of Soviet-German hegemony (as in the 1920s, though now with the much greater weight of the Soviet Union behind it). Before the start of the Moscow conference of foreign ministers Secretary of State George Marshall explained the American position to his French opposite number: "We do not fear so much seeing Germany rising again if a genuine agreement of the four powers is established. What we are worried about is a Germany which will ally herself with one or the other of the four associated powers."[116]

As after the First World War, the question of security policy was closely linked to problems connected with reparations and the economy. The policy compromise on reparations that had been reached at the Potsdam Conference was still cooperative in character. However, the one-sided implementation of this agreement by the Soviet Union in its zone of occupation presented the United States with the unacceptable alternative of either consigning Germany to economic chaos (with all the political consequences that this entailed) or feeding the German population for many years to come with American taxpayers' money, thereby making the implementation of the Soviet reparations program possible on a loan basis. This would also have meant that the Germans, with what remained of their industrial capacity, would have worked primarily for reparations delivered to the Soviet Union and not for export (which was necessary to cover the costs of imports of foodstuffs and raw materials). This and the establishment of Soviet trusts in the Soviet zone of occupation would have meant that, at least in economic terms, Germany would have become firmly incorporated into the Soviet sphere of influence. The Soviet Union was asking the United States to make this policy possible with American financial support.

Thus in this area the situation resembled the one after the First World War—although with different opponents. And just as Wilson and his successors had not been prepared to allow Germany to be turned into a French colony by means of reparations regulations, and to finance reparations indirectly via American loans, the American government under Truman now refused to allow Germany to become a Soviet province with American help.[117] In both cases the American government certainly did not want to prevent the states that had suffered most under the German troops from receiving German reparations. Yet such reparations were not to prevent completely the establishment of free and nondiscriminatory trade, and were not to be misused to achieve one-sided control over Germany. Inasmuch as French policy on Germany after 1945 once again displayed similar intentions, American criticisms were not leveled only at Moscow, but also at Paris.

As in the 1920s, the United States (after the influence of the Morgenthau group had been eliminated) was concerned with achieving the economic stabilization and reintegration of Germany. Furthermore, the similarity of the two postwar situations was perceived as such by leading American politicians. Among those who contended that the post–World War I experience had shown that the reconstruction of Europe was inextricably linked with the use of German industrial potential, and that a deindustrialization of Germany would create chaos throughout Europe and a global trade imbalance that would also affect the United States, were Secretary of War Henry Stimson and his closest aides, Secretary of the Navy James Forrestal, John Foster Dulles (the foreign policy adviser of the Republican presidential candidate), General Lucius Clay and his political adviser Ambassador Robert Murphy, and businessmen such as Alfred Sloan of General Motors. They also said that the destruction of industrial production in Germany ran counter to the interests of American corporations, and that to compensate for this by erecting production plants in other European countries was not an attractive proposition.[118] The advocates of the reintegration concept—as in the 1920s—consciously accepted the reestablishment of German competition in order to create a free trade system that was in the interests of all states. Thus the State Department declared on December 12, 1945: "The United States does not seek to eliminate or weaken German industries of a peaceful character, in which Germany has produced effectively for world markets, for the purpose of protecting American markets from German goods, aiding American exports, or for any other selfish advantage."[119]

At the same time this official declaration was, of course, directed against attempts by any other country to misuse the plan to dismantle the armaments industries agreed to in Potsdam for its own trade policy ends at the expense of German industry of a peaceful nature.

For many years thereafter the destruction of industries that were of significance for the armaments sector remained part of American policy on Germany. This was coupled with the rejection of the Soviet reparations program, and with the overall goal "to see Germany's economy geared to the world system and not an autarchical system."[120] In the phase leading from antagonistic cooperation to the Cold War, the United States, in its policy on Germany, also maintained a "schizophrenic attitude" toward the Soviet Union that the State Department's Committee on Foreign Aid described as "solidarity forever if at all possible, but a well protected flank if not."[121]

After the Soviet Union had rejected both the four-power treaty and a new and comprehensive compromise on reparations at the conference of foreign ministers in Moscow, the continuation of cooperation between the great powers and the implementation of the universalist American policy in Europe and Germany were clearly out of the question. The fronts were obvious, and prefigured a new transatlantic arrangement, namely, within a bipolar global system.

This finally also ruled out the possibility of implementing the fundamentally different concept of a federation taking in the *whole* of Europe that would have been a third force between the superpowers, the United States and the Soviet Union. Carrying on the pan-European ideas of the 1920s, this concept, in a variety of guises, had been developed and propagated by noncommunist resistance groups in all West European countries, by the German resistance movement, and among German exiles. The system of rival and sovereign nation-states was not to be reinstated in liberated Europe after victory over Nazi Germany, which had forcibly united Europe by conquest, "like the fisherman bringing together the fish in his net," and a European federation was to take its place. The incorporation of a federal Germany or of individual German states in a European federation seemed to be the best solution to the "German question."[122]

This pan-European peace program was advocated by the federalist associations, which united in 1946 to form the Union of European Federalists. They continued to oppose the resurrection of national governments. As the new structure of power involving the two superpowers emerged with greater clarity, it increasingly seemed as if a European federation was the sole alternative to Russo-American condominium or the division of Europe into spheres of superpower influence. Whereas associations that were largely middle-class in character (such as the Swiss "Europa Union") strove for close cooperation with the United States with regard to economic and cultural affairs, federalists who were socialists tended in ideological terms to maintain an equidistant attitude to the United States and the Soviet Union. They believed that a united Europe should pursue a third path that lay between American imperialism and Soviet-style communism.

After the process of bipolarization that led to the Cold War had come to an end, the European federalists were forced to change their pan-European proposal for a third force and path: they were compelled to restrict their federalist concept to Western Europe and, in terms of order and security policy, to incorporate a federal Western Europe into the East-West conflict on the side of the United States. This united Western Europe was not a third force pursuing a third path, but engaged in the formation of a joint counterpoise together with and under the leadership of the United

States, which in real political terms now provided the decisive impetus for the integration of Western Europe.

8. THE TRANSATLANTIC ALLIANCE IN THE COLD WAR

With the advent of the Cold War, the East-West polarization that had been anticipated in the nineteenth century became of decisive international importance. It had already existed in a rudimentary way in terms of realpolitik after 1917, although under the conditions of a multipolar division of power. In political terms this had now changed to become bipolarity.[123] The communist threat as perceived in Western Europe and the United States now no longer came from a weak state, but from the second-largest great power (and one that was soon to acquire nuclear weapons). The reply to this was the formation of a transatlantic counterpoise and its subsequent institutionalization in the Cold War. President Truman described this "grand design" as "the building of power balance sufficient to destroy the debilitating fear of Soviet aggression and then, from this secure power base, taking active measures, on the one hand to remove in the non-Soviet world the social and economic pressures on which communism thrives, and on the other hand to create active counterpressure to undermine the base of Soviet power itself."[124] All other diverging goals—as President Truman reminded his European allies—were to be subordinated to this common policy, "to the overriding necessity of evolving a realistic workable policy to insure, first, our survival, and, second, the eventual triumph of the West." With this third transatlantic war coalition the bipolar concept attained its purest form—a polarity of power and order with an institutionalized transatlantic alliance that was a community of interests and values directed against the communist superpower.

The American idea of a universalist order was asserted throughout the world in contradistinction to the Soviet Union and its sphere of influence. However, initially the concept was capable of being implemented only in the West, and only in a contradictory manner involving a number of compromises (discussed below). Thus institutionalized cooperation in the field of monetary and trade policy had to be reduced. The economic aid and reconstruction program, the Marshall Plan, which had been designed for the whole of the Continent, had to be restricted to Western

Europe—with the Organization for European Economic Cooperation (OEEC) as an institutionalized framework and with insistence on the most-favored-nation principle in West European states (this was wholly in keeping with the policy pursued by Hull). Finally, the concept of the four-power treaty, similarly reduced, was transformed into the military Atlantic alliance (NATO). It was an instrument of dual containment: against the new threat and against the recurrence of the old one.

In this new pattern of transatlantic relations it was of the greatest importance that the United States—which was clearly the hegemonic power in the transatlantic alliance because of its economic and military strength (initially with a monopoly on and later with a lead in nuclear weapons)—did not, in contrast to the attitude adopted in the 1920s and 1930s, regard organized cooperation among the European states as being against its interests. On the contrary, it now called for—and, indeed, encouraged—West European federation or integration, and even provided *governmental* financial support. This was the greatest innovation, and the most important element of discontinuity in a situation that was otherwise characterized by the recurring necessity of transatlantic counterpoise formation and the renewed implementation of the new American doctrine (now globalized in the shape of the Truman Doctrine).

Like the multilateral economic aid program, the idea of establishing a European federation after the Second World War instead of restoring the rival European nation-states had been the subject of lively debate in the United States even before the Cold War. None other than John Foster Dulles, in his capacity as chairman of the Commission on a Just and Durable Peace of the Federal Council of Churches, had argued as early as September 1941 that "a federated continental Europe" was in both European and American interests. Only such a structural change in the anarchical European system of states would make it possible to prevent new wars, into which the United States would inevitably be drawn, and avert the utter destruction of Europe. "Europe must federate or perish."[125]

However, as we have seen, at the end of the war this concept was neither American nor European policy. Only when the problem of dual containment occurred did the concept of federalization determine American policy on Europe, even though it was restricted to Western Europe. In a much-publicized speech to the National Publishers Association in New York on January 17, 1947, which was based on the leitmotif cited above,

Dulles, who in the meantime had become the foreign policy adviser to the Republican presidential candidate, combined a case for a policy of containment of Soviet expansionist aims with the concept of federalism. American policy on Germany was to contribute to its realization, and at the same time it was supposed to solve the German question. Dulles conceded: "Of course, the German settlement will not of itself bring a federation of Europe. Only the European people themselves can do that, and they probably will move slowly. But the German settlement will decisively determine whether the movement will be toward economic unification or toward rebuilding the old structure of independent, unconnected sovereignties."[126] The reestablishment of a united Germany with exclusive control over German economic potential would not be tolerated by its Western neighbors: "If the industrial potential of western Germany cannot be safely integrated into Western Europe, it ought not to be fully used by Germans alone." In this case deindustrialization would be a logical measure, though this could not create permanent security. Thus Dulles concluded that only a federalization of Europe that included Germany would make possible a development of the industrial potential of West Germany in the interests of Western Europe (including Germany), and that such joint control would make the reconstruction of Germany possible without turning the Germans into the masters of Europe.

After the failure of the Moscow foreign ministers conference, Secretary of State Marshall adopted this federalization concept and made it the basis of his European aid program, which, after the failure of the bilateral aid programs, was devised on multilateral lines.[127] The Congress even wished to make a European federation a precondition for American economic aid. With the Marshall Plan alternative, plans for a separate reconstruction of western Germany that had been propagated by former President Herbert Hoover and others became obsolete. However, the West European states still had to be persuaded to adopt the concept, and here the German problem was of strategic significance.

The intensity with which this work of persuasion was carried out in 1948 and 1949 by Secretary of State Marshall, European Recovery Program Special Ambassador Averell Harriman, and numerous other governmental and social actors is impressively demonstrated by the sources, although it cannot be documented in the present context. It culminated in the "lesson in power politics" that the American president and his secretaries of state and defense gave to the foreign ministers of the European states of the alliance on the eve of the signing of the NATO treaty.[128]

The American leadership had the impression that no other international issue led to more serious differences of opinion between the new alliance partners than policy on Germany and Japan. For this reason Secretary of State Dean Acheson spelled out the American position very clearly: "We see Japan and Germany as major power centers, neutralized now but inevitably reviving, lying between the U.S.S.R. and the West. There is no question but that the U.S.S.R. looks upon the eventual absorption of Germany, in particular, into the Soviet orbit as a major objective. . . . From the Western point of view, we too realize the grave dangers of encouraging German revival. We believe, however, that the advantages of orienting Germany toward the West and countering Soviet moves justify a calculated risk. Any Allied policy which does not allow reasonable scope for German revival may force that nation into the arms of the U.S.S.R. Therefore, we urge that the Western powers adopt a joint policy of encouraging German economic revival, accelerating the development of democratic institutions, and actively combatting Soviet subversion." The objections of the European foreign ministers were rather muted. French Foreign Minister Robert Schuman continued to regard "perpetual neutralization" as the "ideal solution," especially since the Soviet Union would no doubt be in agreement with it. British Foreign Minister Ernest Bevin noted that a British "essential" was nationalization of the German economy (but this was blocked by the United States) and expressed fears of economic competition. Acheson rejected it all. It turned out that the idea of European integration and Germany's incorporation in a federal Europe was of decisive importance for the formation of a transatlantic consensus, for in this way it was possible to combine partnership with control.

But apart from policy on Germany, from an American point of view the economic and political unification of Western Europe was "an equally important corollary to all-out defense cooperation," which materialized with the foundation of NATO, because only thus was it possible to create a "power balance" without prohibitive cost: "Dovetailing of the European economies and closer political cooperation will have two effects. By establishing a solid base for recovery it will both reduce the internal communist threat and provide the essential power base for adequate future armament. Europeans must recognize that the prewar economic situation is gone forever." Acheson noted disapprovingly that after the initial impulse provided by the European Recovery Program (later known as the Marshall Plan), the momentum of European cooperation had slowed down, and he demanded progress toward integration.

Thus the grand U.S. design to form a transatlantic counterpoise to the Soviet Union was based on comprehensive military integration, with the United States, Britain, and France as the "genuine combined command," and on the economic and political integration of Western Europe, including the newly established state of the Federal Republic of Germany. To make things easier for West European states, the United States was prepared to concentrate its global containment policy (the Truman Doctrine) in Europe (the "decisive theater is Western Europe"). In return the United States required the West Europeans to adopt its policies on Germany and Europe, and to amend their colonial policies (in other words, to relinquish "the forlorn attempt to reestablish prewar patterns of colonial domination").

As to decolonization, that process was determined more by events in the colonies themselves than by American pressure. As to the policy on Germany and Europe, France finally decided to make the best of it by becoming the initiator of continental European integration with the Schuman Plan, which French historian Raymond Poidevin rightly described as a result of the Marshall Plan.[129] (Similarly, the Locarno Pact had been the result of the Dawes Plan.) The Marshall Plan was, so to speak, the new American economic peace for Europe, and the Schuman Plan its Franco-German specification in Western Europe (whereas Britain wished to retain its special position and for this reason opposed further moves for the development of the OEEC). It was a Pax Franco-Germanica within the Pax Americana. In this sense the French policy of integration was a positive reaction to American policy on Europe and Germany, and at the same time one that was designed to preserve French power. With the Schuman Plan the French not only pursued the goal of protecting their own economic power base against independent German competition, but also attempted "to restore their own position with the Americans, guard their leadership in Western Europe and defuse the dangers they perceived in the growing 'special relationship' between Bonn and Washington."[130]

The Monnet memorandum of May 3, 1950, which defined the Schuman Plan in internal terms, shows that in this new French policy on Europe and Germany, the idea of the formation of a counterpoise in the

Cold War and the involvement of Germany also played the decisive role, although at the same time the intention was to create a European counterpoise to American hegemony within the transatlantic alliance.[131] A similar idea underlay the Pleven Plan, namely, controlling German armed forces through a European Defence Community and functioning within NATO as the leading EDC power.

From the point of view of leading American politicians, the creation of a European power factor (for the purposes of burden-sharing) was certainly in the interests of the United States in order to diminish the American "burdens of bipolarity."[132] At the time of the founding of NATO, as the above consultations demonstrate, a tripartite leadership consisting of the United States, Britain, and France (and coordination through European organizations) had been envisaged; and as is well known, the United States fully supported the EDC concept until it failed to pass the French National Assembly. Thus it was not merely the situational need to form a countervailing power in the Cold War, but fundamental ideas on the structural maintenance of peace that determined support for the policy of European federalization in the case of responsible American politicians such as John Foster Dulles and George Kennan. It was logical that the United States should subsequently have supported the foundation of the European Economic Community (EEC) and of Euratom, which represented the continuation of European integration in the economic sphere.[133]

This policy implied that even in the transatlantic relationship the United States was able to implement its idea of a multilateral and liberal order only in a modified manner. For a decade it accepted the existence of what amounted to two currency blocs instead of the single Bretton Woods monetary system: the European Payments Union with its non-European franc and sterling currency areas on the one hand, and the dollar zone on the other.[134] If the EDC (and the EPU) had materialized, NATO multilateralism—which, because of American predominance, constituted de facto American hegemony—would have been transformed into Euro-American bilateralism. The United States took the risk of allowing the EEC to develop into an economic and trade union that contained elements of discrimination toward the United States. This was acceptable under the conditions of "hegemonic cooperation."[135]

Thus the new relationship between Western Europe and the United States was based on a dual structure: the transatlantic security community and the European economic community. The inherent tension between the two could become an acute political problem.

In the context of the Cold War the United States was the decisive balancer against the Soviet Union; in the transatlantic relationship, the balancer and "pacifier" among the European states (particularly as a counterpoise to a resurgent Germany).[136] And at the same time it exercised hegemony in the transatlantic alliance through the Supreme Allied Commander in Europe, the command structure of the integrated armed forces organization that was set up after the Korean War.

In 1939 and 1940, in order to prevent and survive the Pax Germanica, Britain had chosen the Pax Americana. Faced with the choice of a Pax Sovietica or a Pax Americana, the West European states again chose the latter because this was the only way of ensuring their survival. On the basis of a democratic value community it was possible to introduce elements of partnership into the hegemonic relationship ("security community") because European integration offered opportunities for a genuine European policy and for a symmetrical pattern of Euro-American relations in the future.[137] As time went on, this complex functional pattern of transatlantic relations—which was the result of the bipolar distribution of power and the bipolarizing effect of the East-West conflict, and at the same time included a tendency to multipolarity—assumed different forms. These were dependent on the ways in which the East-West conflict was regulated, and on the shifts of power in the East-West and transatlantic relationships.

9. TRANSATLANTIC RELATIONS DURING THE PERIOD OF DÉTENTE

As long as the Soviet threat remained, and as long as it could be countered only by means of the alliance between the West European states and the United States, the preconditions for continuity in the transatlantic alliance were basically unchallenged. A further element of continuity was the enduring need to integrate the Federal Republic of Germany into the Atlantic alliance. However, elements of change modified this situational continuity and the resultant directional continuity of the common policy of balancing.

The fundamental changes that began to emerge toward the end of the 1950s, and that were increasingly anticipated and then materialized in the

1960s, were on the one hand the increase in the Soviet Union's nuclear and military potential until it reached parity and attained a secure second-strike capacity, and on the other the increase in the economic power of Western Europe and, in this context, the rise of the Federal Republic to the status of an economic power. Outside the North Atlantic area the development of the People's Republic of China as a competitor and counterpoise to the Soviet Union, the rise of Japan to the status of an economic power, and the organization of the Third World states (Nonaligned Movement) introduced further fundamental shifts of power that in turn affected the transatlantic relationship.

The new strategic nuclear balance of power meant that in the event of a major war, the United States would be threatened with nuclear annihilation, and thus in the case of limited, local, or regional attacks in Europe doubt began to be cast on the credibility of American nuclear deterrence. American and European interests could diverge, and the choice between massive retaliation (which would have resulted in self-destruction) and surrender was unbearable. Both the Berlin crisis triggered in 1958 by the Soviet Union and the Berlin and Cuba crises of 1961–63 focused attention on these changes—on both sides of the Atlantic. Thus the regulation of the East-West conflict, and the strategy and internal relations of the Atlantic alliance had to be adjusted to the changes in the balance of power that had occurred.

The partial détente that President John F. Kennedy initiated with Soviet Party Chairman Nikita Khrushchev, and the policy of détente that President Richard Nixon and his national security adviser and then secretary of state, Henry Kissinger, pursued with Leonid Brezhnev, constituted a policy of containment with new means, a regulation of the East-West conflict that entailed the inclusion of cooperative elements into the system of power and countervailing power formation.[138] The idea was the cooperative stabilization of the antagonistic East-West system and of Mutual Assured Destruction (MAD) by means of cooperative arms control and by the creation of a political modus vivendi. The recognition of the status quo that this implied was aimed, it is true, at its abolition in the long term. But as the first negotiated East-West agreements (such as the Partial Test Ban Treaty and the Nonproliferation Treaty) demonstrate, in the short and medium term, structures were created that cemented the division of Europe and of Germany. The joint American-Soviet Declaration on Basic Principles and the May 1973 Strategic Arms Limitation Talks Agreements (SALT I), and the 1973 American-Soviet treaty on the prevention of a nuclear war marked the high points of bilateral superpower détente.

The strategy of the Atlantic alliance and the relationship between its European and North American members was adjusted with a great deal of difficulty to the new strategic nuclear balance of power and to the ensuing U.S. policy of détente. This happened in two stages and at two crucial points, 1966–67 and 1973–74. On both occasions the alternative to the Atlantic solution was formulated and backed by France, and on both occasions the Federal Republic was the strategically decisive factor. It was the linchpin, not only with regard to the East-West relationship, but also regarding the structure of the transatlantic relationship.

The First Process of Adjustment

The economic and social structure of the Federal Republic of Germany, more than that of any other West European country, was shaped by the Marshall Plan (which in turn was based on fundamental aspects of American occupation policy) and by the ensuing private investment (which was able to capitalize on American involvement in the 1920s). The reformist neocapitalist cooperation between the state, employers, and unions (three-cornered partnership)—and the social partnership concept of increased productivity as an alternative to class struggle and the redistribution of wealth, which in the opinion of the American unions was what was really being exported by the Marshall Plan—was implemented in an ideal manner in Germany.[139] Coalitions between American and German businessmen and trade unionists now materialized, and these were of the greatest significance for political stabilization in Germany and between Germany and the United States. They were the intersocietal complementation of cooperation between the two governments. In economic and trade terms this was the result of coinciding interests in liberal world trade; in security policy it was the result of the divided country's vital dependence on American protection and of the strategic significance of Germany as a border area in the context of the American policy of containment of the systemic opponent.[140]

The fact that economic reintegration, initiated by the Marshall Plan, occurred through the institutionalization of European integration meant that in terms of trade policy, the Federal Republic became increasingly dependent on the EEC rather than on the United States. And relations between the EEC and the United States developed in a highly contradictory manner. The United States made use of the larger market by increasing its direct investments, and in Europe (as in the 1920s) this led to fears of "Americanization" or even "American colonialism." Meanwhile, the United States considered EEC agricultural policy and the preferential treatment of Africa and the Mediterranean area discriminatory and detrimental to its export interests.[141] It tried to use the 1961–62 and 1964–67 rounds of General Agreement on Tarrifs and Trade (GATT) negotiations to force the EEC to adopt its liberal global trade policy, and even resorted to strategies of conflict (such as the "chicken war"). On the other hand, the *défi américain* (or American challenge) led the French government to the conclusion that European economic integration urgently needed a political superstructure in the shape of federal or confederal institutions, for only then would it be possible, as French Prime Minister Mendès-France put it, to create "the basic preconditions for the independence of Europe from the United States." Clearly, the issue at stake was the formation of an economic counterpoise within the transatlantic relationship.[142]

As a result of the changes in the strategic nuclear East-West relations referred to earlier, the economic differences acquired an enhancement in the field of security policy. The establishment of an independent French nuclear capacity (the *force de frappe*), which had already been decided during the Fourth Republic, was designed to close the growing credibility gap in the American security guarantee and at the same time to give France a leadership function in a confederated Western Europe.

After he had returned to power in the Fifth Republic, French President Charles de Gaulle used these factors to forge the concept of a European third force situated between the two superpowers. Its stated aim was to unite Western Europe under French leadership, and then to reach a compromise with Russia on overcoming the division of Europe, and to establish an equal and balanced partnership with the United States in the place of American hegemony. Thus it was a refurbished version of the three-cornered concept that had already been mooted in the nineteenth century, and that had been propounded in modified form by Briand in 1929–30.

Yet under the constraints of the East-West conflict, and as long as the Soviet threat persisted, the presence of the U.S. strategic nuclear umbrella and the continuation of the transatlantic alliance were still necessary, even in de Gaulle's opinion. After all, the *force de frappe* could perform its function only under this umbrella—that is, to trigger in time nuclear retaliation if the Soviet Union chose to attack in Europe. But precisely this function ran counter to American interests and to the strategy of flexible and centralized response to be controlled from Washington. The geopolitical position of the Federal Republic meant that it—like France—had an interest in dissuading the Soviet Union from limited aggression in Europe by means of a credible threat of early nuclear retaliation.[143]

De Gaulle initially attempted to transform NATO on French terms by creating a tripartite leadership (United States, Britain, and France), although this was rejected by America (and Britain), partly on account of its strategic ally, Germany.[144] As a result, the French president concluded that a West European continental power grouping *including* the Federal Republic would have to be created before an Atlantic alliance and relations with Russia could be restructured on tripartite lines. After the failure of the so-called Fouchet Plans, this strategy was reduced to the creation of a Franco-German union as the core of a European confederation. The 1963 Franco-German Friendship Treaty (or Elysée Treaty) was intended to serve this purpose.[145]

Federal Chancellor Konrad Adenauer also understood West European integration with France as a means of preserving peace between the European states, as a counterpoise to the Soviet Union, and as the core of a third force. His assessment of the change in the strategic nuclear balance of power and its effect on the American security guarantee for Europe was similar to that of de Gaulle. As it became apparent that the solution he preferred—turning NATO into an independent nuclear power—was unattainable, he came to see the *force de frappe* as a positive European deterrence factor under the American nuclear umbrella. Furthermore, the French policy of détente, in contrast to its American counterpart, was linked not to the stabilization of the status quo in Europe, but to its replacement by a pan-European order, and this would have meant the end of the division of Germany. Finally, firmly institutionalized cooperation with France corresponded to the German interest in preventing a Franco-Soviet rapprochement at the expense of Germany, and the French interest in precluding a German-Soviet rapprochement. A common Franco-German ostpolitik and a common policy toward the United States was the Gaullist alternative to the continuation of American hegemony in Western Europe and Soviet rule over Eastern and Central Europe.[146]

However, the Gaullist policy on the new West European and Atlantic order came to grief on account of the "Atlanticists" in Western Europe and stiff resistance from the United States. The Fouchet Plans were blocked by the Dutch;[147] and the Franco-German treaty was reinterpreted by German Atlanticists in the Adenauer government (Gerhart Schröder and Ludwig Erhard), who had the support of the Social Democratic Party (SPD) opposition and of the broad pro-American societal coalition that underpinned the German-American relationship in material and ideal terms in a transnational way.[148] However, the existential dependence of the Federal Republic on the United States in terms of security policy was the decisive factor. The American nuclear deterrent could at the most be complemented, but not replaced, by the French *force de frappe*. Furthermore, the Atlanticists close to Erhard, who succeeded Adenauer as chancellor in 1963, were united with the American government in their strict rejection of French hegemony.[149] For a long time both governments considered the establishment of a multilateral nuclear capacity within NATO the best way of meeting the German request to participate in nuclear deterrence and defense (and thus to ensure the continued integration of the Federal Republic into the West), and at the same time preventing the advent of French hegemony or the formation of a Franco-German bloc in Europe.[150] The Americans acted in accordance with their traditionally defined interests, according to which any kind of hegemony in Europe was detrimental to the United States. In this respect they were acting in the tradition of the policy on Europe of the 1920s. And the German Atlanticists preferred, for security and trade reasons, a modified American hegemony within the Atlantic alliance to French hegemony.

The results of this test of strength were as follows.[151] The United States was unable to stop de Gaulle from establishing an independent nuclear capacity, from taking France out of the integrated military structure of the alliance (as of July 1, 1966), and from preventing Britain from joining the EEC (which the United States supported, with a view to encouraging pro-Atlanticist EEC policies). Meanwhile, de Gaulle was unable to prevent the adjustment of NATO policies in 1967, largely in accordance with American wishes. The strategy of massive retaliation was replaced by that of flexible response (with minor modifications in regard to the role played by tactical nuclear weapons). The control of and decision to use nuclear weapons remained in American hands. As a concession to the nonnuclear European members of the alliance, and especially to the Federal Republic (after the failure of the plans for a multilateral nuclear force, or MLF, which were primarily designed to meet German wishes for participation), a nuclear planning group was established in which Germany and Italy were permanent members. In other words, participation in planning was institutionalized, though not in decision-making.

Finally, after the so-called Harmel report, the alliance was deliberately incorporated into the policy of détente.[152] The policy of balancing and the policy of détente were now defined as mutually complementary functions, and a new peaceful order for the whole of Europe (including an end to the division of Germany) was projected as a long-term aim of the alliance. This then was the document that defined the active role of the Atlantic alliance in the policy of détente and arms control in Europe (the Conference on Security and Cooperation in Europe, or CSCE, and the Mutual and Balanced Force Reduction). It was also possible to integrate into this concept the bilateral German ostpolitik, which began to emerge at the same time and was implemented in 1970 by means of the treaties with Germany's eastern neighbors. In fact, in this way it was brought under the control of the alliance.[153] A central Europe concept, which was propagated for a time by Egon Bahr, the chief architect of the new German ostpolitik, and was designed to replace NATO, had little chance of being implemented under these circumstances (quite apart from Soviet opposition to the scheme).[154]

All in all NATO emerged strengthened from the adjustment crisis. A "dual track" structure was established, "which in one case involved all members of NATO, and in the other only those that participated in the integrated defense program" (for example, excluding France, for certain periods Greece, and from 1986 onward Spain).[155] Even after the establishment of the Euro-Group as a European consultative and coordination body, and of the Independent Defense Planning Group (in which France participated), this structure was far removed both from the ideas of de Gaulle and from Kennedy's vision of an "Atlantic Partnership" with two pillars, one of which was American and the other European.[156] The U.S. claim to leadership and its nuclear decision-making monopoly were difficult to reconcile with the partnership concept. On the part of the Americans the latter was construed merely as something that might materialize in the future, and was tied to preconditions that were difficult to comply with. It would be possible to concede a degree of participation only after the establishment of a European political entity and only in the event of interests shared by the United States and such a United States of Europe. And the decision on when and whether both preconditions had been fulfilled remained the preserve of the United States.[157]

In reality, in the 1960s the United States continued to be the hegemonic power, even after the adjustment in 1967, and the transatlantic alliance continued to be a hegemonic relationship. To be sure, it was what has been termed a "mild kind of hegemony," with cooperative structures within the transatlantic alliance, and with the perspective of a cooperative balance-of-power policy toward the systemic opponent.

The Second Process of Adjustment

In 1973 and 1974 the need for a renewed adjustment of the Atlantic alliance resulted from a further shift in the economic balance of power between the United States and the West European alliance partners (and Japan), and from the desire of the EEC states (which now included Britain) to pursue the process of integration—including the intergovernmental coordination and streamlining of foreign policy through European Political Cooperation (EPC). U.S. economic weakness as a result of the Vietnam War had consequences with regard to budgetary and monetary policy, which were merely postponed for a number of years by the Federal Republic's currency compensation payments (made in return for the import of American security). In August 1971 the United States unilaterally and quite suddenly decided to abandon the gold standard and the convertibility of the dollar, and at the same time placed a surcharge on foreign imports. With this, the Bretton Woods global monetary system that had been established and led by the United States collapsed, and the United States (temporarily) ignored the GATT system.[158]

The national currency policy pursued by the United States reinforced the efforts on the part of the West European states to coordinate their monetary policy (for example, the European "currency snake"and "block floating" against the dollar). Linked to this was the idea that it was possible not only to define European "identity" but also to play an independent role in global politics, although, because of the persistent Soviet threat and the strategic nuclear balance provided by the United States, without relinquishing the Atlantic alliance.

After it had stabilized its détente relationship with its antagonist, the Soviet Union, the American government reacted by attempting to stabilize its relationship with its European allies, to preserve the basic hegemonic structure by making certain adjustments, to integrate a "nascent Europe" into the global American concept, and to exercise control over the EEC through the transatlantic alliance.

This was how, in April 1973, Henry Kissinger interpreted the initiative to make 1973 the "year of Europe" and to regulate transatlantic relations with a new Atlantic Charter. His intention was to formulate a joint declaration that restated the differentiated roles that had been valid up to that point (the global role of the United States, the regional role of the West European states) and emphasized the "linkage" between the maintenance of the American security guarantee and a European quid pro quo in the economic sphere and with regard to military burden-sharing.[159]

Kissinger's initiative led to bitter diplomatic wrangles between the United States and the West European states, with France as the most determined opponent of the United States. These transatlantic debates were exacerbated by the escalation of the Middle East conflict (particularly the Yom Kippur War) and the Arab challenge (notably the oil embargo and oil price shock).

The Europeans attempted to circumvent the policy of linkage by suggesting that in place of a *single* basic declaration there should be *two* declarations passed separately: an Atlantic declaration and a Euro-American declaration.

The EPC draft agreement that was presented to the United States in September 1973 contained what amounted to a declaration of the political equality of the EC, and was an attempt to have this recognized by the American government.[160] True, the preamble emphasized common values and drew the lesson from history that the United States and the European states should remain "closely linked." However, the very first phrase expressed quite unmistakably that there should be a "new bilateralism" between Western Europe and the United States (instead of the earlier bilateral relationships between the United States and the various European states):

"The United States of America, on the one hand, and the European Community and its member states, on the other hand . . . undertake to intensify their existing cooperation on an equal basis in accordance with the following principles and to maintain a constructive dialogue."

The principles listed began with a remark that rejected the roles that had been defined by Henry Kissinger: "The United States, recognizing that the creation of the Community is an event of great international importance and has enhanced the stability of Europe, welcomes the intention of the Nine to insure that the Community establishes its position in world affairs as a distinct entity." Only after this American recognition of the EC's role did the draft proceed to formulate certain common principles. Problems of trade and monetary policy were to be dealt with in various distinct separated bodies (GATT, IMF). Questions relating to defense policy were not specifically mentioned. They were to be dealt with in the NATO declaration that was to be issued at the same time, and thus could not be linked to political and economic problems.

The American government considered the draft EPC agreement a provocation, and further developments led to a confrontation between Europe and the United States; as in the 1920s, the beginnings of an independent European policy were assessed in terms of the Europeans' "ganging up" on the United States.[161] Now and during the disagreements in the spring of 1974 concerning energy strategy, the United States brought up the question of the alliance to the Europeans who were beginning to turn against it. It did so both on a diplomatic level and in public. In his famous speech in Chicago on March 15, 1974, President Nixon explained: "Now, the Europeans cannot have it both ways. They cannot have the United States participation and cooperation on the security front and then proceed to have confrontation and even hostility on the economic and political front."[162]

Confronted with this alternative, the European members of the alliance were forced to give in. In contrast to the situation in the 1920s, Western Europe was no longer dependent on the inflow of American capital, but on the import of American security. And the state for which this dependence was of existential importance now became the principal architect of a pro-American compromise.[163]

The proposal for a separate Euro-American declaration was dropped, and at a specially convened meeting at Schloss Gymnich near Bonn on

April 20–21, 1974, the EC foreign ministers reached a "gentlemen's agreement." In practical terms it meant that whenever its interests were affected, the United States would be able to participate in the European decision-making process *before* EPC decisions were reached, or indeed would be able to veto the decision-making process altogether. This acknowledgment of American leadership was merely camouflaged by the fact that the request for consultation with the United States had to be submitted by an EC member state (and it was not difficult to guess which country would perform this function).[164]

The Atlantic Declaration, which was finalized at the same time, adopted soon after at the meeting of the NATO Council in Ottawa, and solemnly signed by the heads of government in Brussels on June 26, 1974, was also largely based on American ideas.[165] Whereas it confirmed the American security guarantee, it was linked to an obligation by the European alliance partners to assume a fair share of the defense burden. It emphasized the determination to increase comprehensive and timely consultations on common alliance interests, and conceded "that these interests may be affected by an event in other areas of the world." The linkage so urgently requested by the United States was recognized by an expression of intent on the part of the alliance partners to ensure "that their security relationships be strengthened through harmonious relations in the political and economic fields." European fears that the Soviet-American agreement on the prevention of a nuclear war concluded in June 1972 might have an adverse effect on nuclear deterrence in Europe were countered by pointing out that agreements on the prevention of war did not lessen the freedom of the NATO states "to deploy all the means at their disposal [including nuclear weapons] if they were attacked." Finally—and this was the most important innovation—the contribution of the European nuclear arsenals (including the *force de frappe*) was recognized as constituting part of the joint deterrent.

By and large, in 1974 the second process of adjustment ended, as the first had done in 1967, with the reconfirmation *and* weakening of American hegemony. In both processes of adjustment the United States used the Federal Republic as a strategic partner, as it had done in the case of the Weimar Republic, to prevent the formation of an anti-American bloc in Western Europe. In terms of foreign policy Germany was unable to reject the American proposals, for this would have been against its own interests. At the same time, it had to bear in mind what Chancellor Willy Brandt had referred to as the "entente élémentaire" with France and its interest in the development of the EC (factors it did not have to consider in the 1920s). For this reason a "balanced" policy was pertinent. This led to a tendency to look for compromise solutions, which in crucial areas had, of course, to correspond to the real distribution of power in the Euro-American relationship and especially in the East-West relationship. In other words, such compromises had to be asymmetrical and in favor of the United States. These positive effects of American-German bilateralism (from an American point of view) encouraged influential politicians and advisers such as C. Fred Bergsten (who was economic adviser in the U.S. National Security Council from 1969 to 1971) to suggest an American-German dual leadership ("bigemony"). In November 1973 Bergsten told a U.S. congressional committee that "in the near future the foreign policy of the United States in regard to Europe should concentrate more on Germany than on the Common Market."[166] In other words, he suggested an orientation to Germany as in the period of stability at the end of the 1920s.

Although a situation that resembled the 1920s (the tendency in Europe to form a West European bloc) led to a similar American policy (the use of the German dependence on America and partially coinciding interests in precluding such developments), the difference was profound. On the one hand the indispensable strategic nuclear presence of the United States, and American balancing of the systemic opponent, the Soviet Union, placed obvious constraints on the West European goal of independence. On the other hand, in the economic sphere the decline in the American hegemonic potential and the growth of West European power—above all, the concentration and institutionalization of European economic power within the EC, which grew and became enhanced by the foundation of the European Council—had the effect of changing the structure of the transatlantic relationship. And in terms of security policy, the tendency toward mitigated hegemony continued unabated. Generally speaking, "Europeanization" became the new leitmotif; it was a policy of balancing within the transatlantic relationship.

A truely symmetrical Euro-American relationship first emerged only in the economic sphere, and with the inclusion of Japan it grew to become a global economic leadership triangle. The annual economic summit, which was instituted in 1975, created the quasi-institutionalization of the new collective leadership, which now included seven members (the Group of Seven leading industrialized nations, or G-7). This put an end to the economic hegemony of the United States.[167]

In the field of monetary policy the EC increasingly began to establish itself as an independent actor, especially with the introduction of the European Monetary System (1978–79), which in the eyes of its German and French authors, Helmut Schmidt and Valéry Giscard d'Estaing, was intended as a counterweight to the dollar and the yen. In the transatlantic wing of this monetary leadership triangle, the United States, together with Germany, France, and Britain, pursued a policy of informal cooperative management through the so-called Library Group, a kind of directorate of four within the IMF's Group of Ten.[168]

In political terms this new collective transatlantic leadership finally materialized at the four-power summit meeting in Guadeloupe in January 1979, which in the face of the threat posed by the Soviet Union's new Eurostrategic weapons (SS-20) decided in favor of the NATO two-track policy.[169] On this point, which was of central importance for the Atlantic policy of counterpoise formation and détente, the decision in principle was not taken by the relevant NATO committees. They merely gave concrete shape to and formalized what the four powers had jointly decided. Prior to this the United States had taken a unilateral decision with regard to the neutron bomb, and this had led to considerable irritation in the alliance.[170]

However, in the regulation of relations with the common opponent, the Soviet Union, U.S. strategic nuclear predominance over its three important European allies and within the Atlantic alliance as a whole continued to be clear, and this had practical consequences for East-West negotiations. With regard to security policy "hardware," the United States continued to play a leading role (for example, in the arms control negotiations on conventional forces, MBFR) or was the sole negotiator (for example, SALT I). In the SALT II negotiations the United States even refused to include the problem of the Soviet Union's Eurostrategic weapons (which infuriated Federal Chancellor Schmidt).[171] On the other hand, in the negotiations on security policy "software" and on economic questions, the EC/EPC played an independent role. In the CSCE negotiations, the positions and procedure were defined first in the CSCE subcommittee of the EPC, and then in the NATO caucus or in the NATO meeetings.[172]

At the first CSCE conference the level of agreement both between EPC members and between NATO states was still fairly high, and it was possible to reach agreement on a common policy. With the crisis of détente this changed in both groupings in the follow-up CSCE conferences. In the transatlantic context the instrumentalization of the human rights question was especially controversial. But the CSCE remained important for the transatlantic relationship because its negotiating framework brought all of the West European countries (including the neutral ones) and the North American states (the United States and Canada) together with the East European states and the Eurasian Soviet Union. Furthermore, the CSCE, both in the new period of confrontation and in the ensuing comprehensive détente, which finally led to the end of the East-West conflict, held out the prospect of uniting the whole of Europe (without excluding the United States).[173]

10. TRANSATLANTIC RELATIONS IN THE 1980s: FROM THE SECOND COLD WAR TO THE SECOND DÉTENTE

Three lines of development intersected at the end of the 1970s: the Soviet Union's Eurostrategic arms buildup, to which NATO responded on December 12, 1979, with its two-track policy (deployment of American medium-range weapons after negotiations and subject to the results of such negotiations); the Soviet arms buildup in the field of intercontinental ballistic missiles (ICBMs) with ten multiple warheads, which indicated a serious shift in the balance of power in favor of the Soviet Union because it might have given it a first-strike option; and the increase in the expansion of Soviet power in the Third World as shown by the military intervention in Afghanistan. U.S. acceptance of this comprehensive challenge meant that the cooperative elements of détente conflict regulation were replaced by confrontational elements. The result might be called a second Cold War.

These renewed changes in the balance of power and in conflict regulation were bound, as in the case of the earlier ones, to have an effect on transatlantic relations, and they once again forced the Atlantic alliance to make adjustments. And only five years later there was once again a need to adjust in a different direction. After the restoration of American and transatlantic power in the intercontinental theater and in Europe (through the deployment of Pershing II and cruise missiles), and after Soviet Party Chairman Mikhail Gorbachev's fundamental change of course, a new policy of compromise commenced. It was, so to speak, a second all-embracing period of détente that took in all those areas that had been excluded in the first period of détente (especially the conflicts in the Third World and the ideological dimension); as to arms control, its aim was not only the limitation but the reduction of strategic nuclear weapons.[174]

In both processes of adjustment, which cannot be described in detail in the present context, differentiation within the Atlantic relationship increased as a result of the different geopolitical situations of the United States and its West European allies, and of the continuing need for U.S. nuclear deterrence. To counter the effects of such differentiation the United States—as early as the last months of Jimmy Carter's presidency, and then more forcefully under Presidents Ronald Reagan and George Bush—attempted to revive American hegemony in place of the collective leadership that had only just been instituted. In other words, the United States sought to restore its hegemonic position in the Atlantic alliance while rebuilding its military strength vis-à-vis the common systemic opponent. There was to be less "decision-sharing," and more "burden-sharing."[175] The hegemonic predilection of the United States to take unilateral decisions and then expect its European allies to follow its lead strengthened the resolve of the West European allies to intensify and expand West European cooperation (which in turn was based on Franco-German cooperation), and to develop independent initiatives toward the systemic opponent. The crisis in East-West relationships and the effects of transatlantic differentiation coincided with a new economic crisis, which had been initiated by the second oil price shock at the end of the 1970s and exacerbated by the economic effects of increased defense expenditure. This led to the emergence of a transatlantic conflict syndrome. It was easy to identify the symptoms, although they were difficult to deal with.[176]

As a result of the détente crisis and the new spirit of confrontation, the West European states—especially the Federal Republic (because of its all-German responsibilities and in deference to the so-called peace movement, with which large sections of the ruling SDP sympathized)—attempted to salvage some of the purported "achievements" of the policy of détente.[177] They adopted the American policy of sanctions with some hesitation and certainly not unanimously, wishing to continue the economic and trade links with Eastern Europe for the purpose of moderation and damage limitation, and to achieve an arms control solution to the problem of medium-range missiles by signaling a willingness to compromise. In short, it was an attempt to keep European East-West relations as far as possible from the global political confrontation and to prevent a policy of "horizontal escalation" of the kind that had been discussed in the U.S. Department of Defense.[178] In terms of economic and monetary policy this overall security policy approach was in line with the striving to protect Western Europe from the negative effects of Reagan's policies and to persuade the United States to change its high interest rate policy (which was designed to finance the American arms buildup by means of inflows of foreign capital). Meanwhile, the United States demanded the support of the West European alliance partners and the inclusion of European relations in the global pattern of the East-West conflict. The Americans objected to the continuation of trade with Eastern Europe. They prepared also to face up to the failure of the arms control negotiations and, after the Polish situation came to a head in 1981–82, wanted to close the gaps on the economic sanctions front.

At and after the Versailles economic summit in June 1982 the irreconcilable nature of these positions suddenly became clear. The Euro-American compromise—American concessions in the monetary sector, and European concessions with regard to East-West trade (although this did not include the cancellation of the major gas pipeline deal with the Soviet Union that had just been concluded)—was immediately interpreted in completely different ways by the Americans and Europeans, and was not implemented. In fact, the conflict worsened because President Reagan, a few days after the Versailles summit, unilaterally and without consultation extended the American ban on exports of equipment needed for the construction of the gas pipelines to American subsidiaries and licensees abroad, thereby violating the sovereignty of the European states. Instead of a trade war with the Soviet Union, there was now the danger of one between Europe and America, and it was possible to avert such an outcome only by retracting the extraterritorial measures adopted by the United States.[179]

More serious still—and now genuinely in the area of security policy—were the effects of President Reagan's surprise announcement of the Strategic Defense Initiative (SDI) on March 23, 1983.[180] This antimissile program called into question the whole idea of nuclear deterrence and the principle of MAD. If it had been implemented, it would have meant asking Western Europe to accept a lower level of security than the United States and, in the event of mutually assured defense on the part of the two superpowers, would have rendered the French and British nuclear weapons worthless.

Reagan's initiative was made public just as the emplacement of the new American medium-range missiles in Germany and Italy was to begin, exacerbating its irritating effect in Europe. Finally, France refused to participate officially in the technological development of SDI, whereas Germany, by participating in it, once again opted for the United States, instead of France. This placed a strain on the recent agreement to expand Franco-German cooperation in the security and defense sector.[181]

At any rate, the deployment of Pershing II and cruise missiles (which was implemented in the Federal Republic by the new chancellor Kohl against vociferous protests from the SPD and the peace movement) led to a reconfirmation and strengthening of the alliance and its capacity to take action. In this way the coupling of the American intercontinental deterrent with European deterrence that had been requested on so many occasions finally materialized. And once again the decision taken by the Federal Republic—which on this occasion was also in line with French interests, and received spectacular support from French President François Mitterrand in the German parliament—had been of crucial importance.[182]

Yet the Americans were ambivalent about this coupling, for it placed constraints on American freedom of action in the case of a European conflict. At the same time it opened up new possibilities, which in their turn were problematic for the Europeans. Under the threat of a drastic reduction of the number of American troops stationed in Europe (the Nunn-Roth amendment to the defense budget for 1984–85), the United States urged the West European members of the alliance to make a significant increase in their conventional defense capacity in order to avoid having to resort to nuclear weapons in the event of a conventional Soviet attack on Europe. At the same time concepts were developed that were designed to facilitate a limited and "victorious" European war with conventional and nuclear weapons—a perspective that, if implemented, would have led to unacceptable levels of destruction on the territory of the Federal Republic. In other words, there continued to be differing interests when it came to the application of the strategy of flexible response.[183]

Weak American leadership under President Carter as well as subsequent attempts to revive American hegemony (which went together with handing over the burdens to the West European partners in the alliance) unintentionally encouraged the development of West European cooperation. "Europe must assert itself" now became the catchphrase.[184] An attempt to do this was made on various levels: through the reactivation of the Western European Union (WEU),[185] increased cooperation within the EC,[186] and intensified Franco-German cooperation (which now extended to the defense sector).[187] Because of its proven loyalty to the alliance (it had implemented NATO policy on missile deployment), the new German government, headed by Helmut Kohl and Hans-Dietrich Genscher—in contrast to its predecessor—was able to pursue this European policy, together with President Mitterrand, without being suspected of anti-Americanism. Nevertheless there were some fears of this kind in the United States. American apprehension that the establishment of a single European internal market might lead to a "Fortress Europe" was countered with the opening of a new round of GATT negotiations (the Uruguay Round), although here the differing interests of Europe and the United States became more apparent than ever.

These developments coincided with the new policy of an all-embracing East-West compromise that had been in progress since the middle of the decade—beginning after Gorbachev had come to power and embarked on a policy of reform, and after Reagan had been reelected and begun to pursue a policy of dialogue (on the basis of a restoration of American power). The adjustments in transatlantic relations resulting from this new policy were easier than the adjustments that were made after the failure of the first period of détente, for now the détente policy approach of the West Europeans once again coincided with the principal approach adopted by the Americans.[188]

Nevertheless, the problems of adjustment were considerable. The Intermediate Nuclear Forces (INF) Treaty, which was signed in Washington on December 7, 1987, produced the "zero solution" for medium-range missiles, and thus removed the threat posed by the SS-20 missiles, which was what the Europeans had demanded. But with this American "coupling," weapons that had just been deployed disappeared, and henceforth the conventional superiority of the Warsaw Pact was an even greater threat to Western Europe. Furthermore, NATO was divided on the question of whether to modernize the remaining short-range weapons. This time the cleavage was not between the United States and the West European states, but between the United States and Britain (whose position was shared by France) on the one hand, and the Federal Republic on the other. The idea that the systemic border running through the middle of Germany was to receive the status of a nuclear "fire break" was not acceptable from a German point of view. However, the Federal Republic was certainly not interested in a complete withdrawal of nuclear weapons from Europe.[189] The controversy was put on ice by means of a temporary compromise, and then became meaningless because of the swift progress made in the area of arms control, which was achieved in the conventional sector under the aegis of the new East-West policy.

The basic military problem of the conventional imbalance in favor of the Warsaw Pact states represented the main threat to Western Europe throughout the East-West conflict, and had been exacerbated by the INF treaty. Now it was finally solved by the negotiations on conventional forces in Europe. The Conventional Forces in Europe Treaty signed at the CSCE summit conference in Paris on November 16, 1990, constituted the major breakthrough that led from the second period of détente to the end of the East-West conflict.[190] It stipulated the supervised asymmetrical reduction of armed forces and the abolition of an invasion capacity (at least in the shape of a large-scale surprise attack), and laid the foundations for the military balance of power in the nascent pan-European order. With this, and despite considerable internal differences, the transatlantic alliance had demonstrated its collective capacity for action, especially in the area of comprehensive détente (although in the critical final phase the central role of American-Soviet superpower bilateralism once more became apparent). As in the case of the negotiations on the INF treaty, the coordination of Western policy took place in a special committee made up of high-ranking representatives of the NATO countries (what had been known as the Special Consultative Group was now the High Level Task Force). In other words, it was pursued collectively. That the CFE treaty was negotiated separately from the CSCE negotiations on confidence-building and security measures, and only between the members of the two pact systems, corresponded to American demands. But France, which wished to highlight the prospect of transcending the blocs, had secured its integration into the "framework of the CSCE." This measure proved to be of great importance. After the collapse of the Warsaw Pact and the Soviet Union, "the CFE treaty, partly on account of its linkage with the continuing CSCE process, was able to survive, and merge into a new security function."[191] By orienting itself in pan-European terms, the transatlantic alliance became an element with a future. The CSCE provided the framework for the stabilizing role played by NATO during the revolutions in Central and Eastern Europe and the collapse of the Soviet Union.

Finally, the greatest structural change in Central Europe—German reunification—provided confirmation of the stabilizing effect of the Atlantic alliance. Conversely, the alliance made the reunification of Germany in freedom possible in the first place.[192] True, NATO did not chair the negotiations, and the CSCE was not the framework in which they took place. This was the conference between the two democratic German states and the four victorious powers of the Second World War (two-plus-four talks). However, the NATO declaration in London on July 6, 1990, was essential to the Soviet Union's accepting the membership of unified Germany in NATO.[193]

What had been one of the purposes of the alliance from the very start—namely, to integrate the Federal Republic and control it on a partnership basis with a policy of "calculated risk" in order to prevent a resurgent Germany from joining forces with the Soviet Union—was now, from a Western point of view (and in part also from an Eastern point of view) given a new lease on life with respect to a greater Germany. President Bush insisted on its membership in NATO as a sine qua non to preclude the potential dangers of a continental Russo-German bloc. This was wholly in keeping with the continuity of American policy on Europe. Britain and France were also adamant about the integration of German power and thus advocated the continuation of the transatlantic alliance to ensure the American presence in Europe and as a guarantor of security.[194] As the Federal Republic—because of its raison d'état, its realistic assessment of the international balance of power, and its internal value preferences—also linked reunification with continuing membership in the alliance, the Soviet Union, which was the loser in the East-West conflict, was urged to give way. This disposed of the possibility of a Russo-German axis.[195] Furthermore, since the Kohl and Genscher government coupled German unification with further moves toward European unification, through the governmental negotiations that led to the Treaty of Maastricht on the European Union, an important precondition for the reordering of the transatlantic relationship after the end of the East-West conflict was established—in close cooperation with France.[196] The Transatlantic Declaration in November 1990 was designed to lead to an institutionalized dialogue between the EC and the United States.[197]

11. TRANSATLANTIC RELATIONS AFTER THE EAST-WEST CONFLICT

A number of conclusions can be drawn from the historical analysis with regard to the situation today, the question of long-term continuity, and the future.

The Current Situation

The end of the East-West conflict has led to the disappearance of structures and processes that the conflict had determined. The bipolar structure of the international system and the bipolarization of international politics—alliance and counteralliance in East and West—are now relics of the past. In the future the overall structure will be determined by a multipolarity with several major powers. This had already developed in an embryonic form, apart from the strategic nuclear bipolarity, in the two preceding decades (above all in the field of economic relations). True, the United States continues to be a superpower ("the world's preeminent power").[198] In fact, since the collapse of the Soviet Union, it has been the only superpower in a position to demonstrate its might on a global basis, and it showed during the Gulf War. "Yet today," as Henry Kissinger has aptly noted, "power is more widely distributed, and the number of conflicts for which military strength is of significance has declined."[199] On this basis Kissinger comes to the conclusion that the new international system will in many respects resemble "the European system of states of the eighteenth and nineteenth centuries." The relatively high level of consensus among the present great powers with regard to ideology and political order (they are all orientated toward democracy and a market economy) in fact suggests a comparison with the Concert of Europe in the nineteenth century.[200]

But in those days the United States was not a member of the concert of great powers. Furthermore, if we bear in mind that today, as a great power, the United States defines its national interest primarily in economic terms,[201] and that economic competition is becoming increasingly important for international relations (thus Edward Luttwak has suggested that geopolitics are being replaced by "geo-economics"), then there are similarities, and perhaps even more noticeable ones, to the multipolar international system of the 1920s—with the profound difference that the United States is no longer the dominant economic power and the Soviet Union no longer exists.[202] But Russia is in a position resembling that of the Weimar Republic (no firmly established democracy, the consciousness of "having been undefeated in battle," and of having been vanquished nonetheless, on top of which there is a revisionist undercurrent in its foreign policy that coexists with dependence on foreign capital and the support of foreign experts).

As after the First World War (and in contrast to the situation after the Second World War), there is no *immediate* hegemonic threat in Europe. In fact the threat to Europe and the United States does not come from the rise of a single power, but from the dissolution of the Soviet empire and of the Soviet Union itself, and from the new conflicts in this area. "Destabilization" (in President Bush's term) and "creeping instability" (in Clinton's) are currently seen to be the common threat. The political fragmentation that came about in 1918 as a result of the defeat of Russia and the dissolution of the Hapsburg monarchy resembles the fragmentation that is the result of the demise of forcible communist integration in the Soviet empire and in Yugoslavia. Once more (as after the two world wars) it is imperative to stabilize Europe and reintegrate both the "vanquished" and the "liberated" states into a new international order.

In all probability Russia will remain a great power, and a nuclear one at that, and it will therefore be necessary to integrate and balance Russia in a cooperative manner. Whether the transatlantic alliance is needed for this, or whether the United States and the West European states are willing to do this within the framework of a common organization is an open question, given that the unifying factor of the existential threat no longer exists. A transatlantic policy of stabilization, as in the 1920s, can also be pursued without a firm alliance. The question of how to incorporate the Central and East European states into the European Union or the WEU and NATO—that is, whether through association and partnership agreements, or through formal membership—is just as open and controversial.

Finally, the "German question," the reliable integration of reunited Germany, is once more at the top of the agenda. After stabilization of the eastern part of the country, its increased power will become apparent (this is already being anticipated in other countries), and thus the problem of balancing or of integrative control will become more acute. Partly because of military constraints (upper limit on armed forces personnel, renunciation of nuclear, biological, and chemical weapons), Germany's power rests on its predominant economic potential, compared with that of other European countries, all of which aggravated the problem of political order. For as long as there is a "pluralist security community" between the Western great powers in which the use of military power is unlikely, power in the "geo-economic" sphere is more important in intra-Western relations than power in the "geopolitical" field. The problem of balance thus exists primarily in that area in which Germany is particularly powerful.

The policy of the "calculated risk," which was deliberately embarked upon when the Atlantic alliance was founded, proved to be the right course of action during the East-West conflict. The Federal Republic became a stable Western democracy, the motor of European integration, and a reliable ally in the containment of the Soviet Union. Now that the main purpose of NATO has been accomplished, with the exception of guarding against the risk of a renewed imperial and expansive policy on the part of Russia, the question arises of whether the secondary (German) purpose of the alliance and its policy of "dual containment" will persist and remain a reason for the continuation of the transatlantic alliance, or whether the integration of Germany in the European Union (and its enlargement to Central and Eastern Europe) will be sufficient. If the second of these alternatives were to be selected, then such a solution of the "German question" would also be a contribution to balanced and cooperative transatlantic relations between the European Union, the United States, and Russia, for Germany would demonstrate its vital interest, in both economic and political terms, in such a cooperative relationship within the EU (as the Federal Republic did in the past). It would correspond roughly to the concept of a cooperative triangle in the North Atlantic–Eurasian area. To continue the geometrical image, the hypotenuse of this cooperation triangle would need to be organized in the manner of an ellipse, with the two focal points, the United States and EU, in the shape of a new transatlantic alliance.[203] All three corners (the United States, EU, and Russia) would be linked by the cooperative circle of the CSCE—interlocking and restraining each other in a co-operative balance (which would become an antagonistic balance of power only in an acute threat situation). The transatlantic alliance would thus constitute the firm basis in this relationship of a "cooperative balance of power"[204] or "competitive cooperation."[205]

Long-Term Continuity

In what direction is the transatlantic policy of the European states or the European Union and the United States (and Russia) likely to move? And will this symmetrical relationship receive support on both sides of the Atlantic, or will other alternatives be advocated?

If, as we search for tentative answers to these questions, we do not wish to allow ourselves to be confused or blinded by rapidly changing assessements that are often determined by the politics of the day, a summary of the transatlantic patterns of action to date and of continuities in the midst of historical change may be useful.

As we have seen, transatlantic relations in the twentieth century were to a large extent dependent on shifts of power, and these were marked by three tendencies:

- — The rise of the Atlantic power, the United States, first to the status of the predominant economic power, and then to that of a superpower laying claim to the right to establish a universal order. This was linked to the decline of Europe. The tendency weakened in the 1960s and 1970s, and became inverted. U.S. economic power declined. Power was enhanced in the West European states through economic integration, and through steps toward a political union.
- — The rise of the peripheral power, Russia, to the status of a communist great power and then to that of an imperial superpower with global revolutionary aims. From 1989 to 1990 the dissolution of this empire and of its core, the Soviet Union, once again (as in 1918) created the problem of how to reintegrate Russia and the East European states into the international system.
- — The thrice-repeated rise of Germany to the status of a great power—with two attempts to acquire a hegemonic position on the Continent

or even global hegemony, both of which ended in failure. The resurgence of Germany and its reintegration into the world community was made possible with American help twice, and on the second occasion integration was underpinned with two kinds of institutional safeguards, an Atlanticist and a European one (NATO and the EEC).

As has been demonstrated in the historical analysis, in the course of shifts of power, alternative patterns of relations between Europe and the United States that had already been discussed in the nineteenth century were implemented in different periods: the bipolar concept, with its two variants of a transatlantic alliance against Germany (together with Russia or the Soviet Union) and a transatlantic alliance against the Soviet Union (together with Germany); the concept of a continental bloc; the Central Europe concept; and the triangular concept. The success or failure of any particular concept was largely dependent on the American position—after the United States had become a world power and had been included into the dialectics of balance of power and hegemony.

However, despite all the changes, there was a large measure of continuity. In other words, in similar recurring situations, the policies by which states responded to it tended to be similar: since the European great powers, as in the earlier European systems of states, were no longer in a position to avert the hegemony of a single state or of a group of states, they repeatedly required the involvement of the United States as a balancing power when once again the threat of hegemony became acute. They preferred a junior partnership with the transatlantic great power to submission to German or Soviet hegemony, and accepted the hegemony of the United States within the Atlantic alliance for the duration of the German or Soviet hegemonic threat in order to ensure national survival, especially since American leadership within the alliance promoted national prosperity and, owing to the democratic value community, was exercised in terms of "benevolent hegemony." At the same time, they tried to strengthen their weight vis-à-vis the predominant power in the alliance, although severe constraints were placed on their attempts at "Europeanization" because they were dependent on the provision of America's balancing against the common threat.

The United States, for its part, considered the hegemonic threat of a single European state to constitute a threat to its security, freedom, and prosperity; in the recurring threat situations the United States was always prepared, in its own interests, to enter into consultations and agreements or even an alliance with the threatened European states in order to avert the impending danger (although it retained the right to decide on the use of military force in general and of nuclear weapons in particular—even in the Washington Treaty of 1949).

This continuity of American policy on Europe—the realist maxim that it was necessary to avert hegemony in Europe—was repeatedly underlined, and in a quite deliberate manner. The New American Doctrine, propounded by Senator and former Secretary of State Knox in 1918, was reiterated several times, in the last place by President Bush in his report on national security strategy in 1990, which states: "[F]or most of this century, the United States has deemed it a vital interest to prevent any hostile power or group of powers from dominating the Eurasian land mass. This interest remains."[206] The historical analysis has shown the extent to which this maxim influenced the direction of foreign policy that was pursued at various points in the twentieth century. All three transatlantic war coalitions were a response to an acute political and military threat by the formation of countervailing power with military means (although in the final case a military test of strength never came about because nuclear weapons deterred both sides from making it).

Furthermore, the antihegemonic maxim was also pursued in a preventive manner, even in cases of potential concentrations of power on the European continent after the acute danger had been successfully overcome. After the First World War the United States was concerned to prevent the formation of a Russo-German bloc just as much as it resisted French hegemony or the formation of a Franco-German bloc. Similarly, the United States effectively resisted British hegemony or the diversion of American resources through British channels. The German central Europe policy of the 1920s and 1930s was also perceived as a threat (as it had been before the First World War), and it evoked American opposition.

After the Second World War there was once again opposition to the formation of a European bloc, without exception to Soviet predominance in Eastern Europe and the potential danger of a Soviet-German concentration of power, and for a time to the formation of a West European bloc under British leadership and the tendency to establish French hegemony over Germany. When, after de Gaulle's return to power, there was a renewed danger of French hegemony or of the formation of a Franco-German bloc, the United States once again responded in an energetic manner, and in doing so had recourse to what de Gaulle termed its German "vassal." And it was not surprising that the Central Europe concept, which resurfaced in a new guise at the start of the period of détente in the planning staff of the German Foreign Ministry, led to a great deal of irritation, especially in the United States.

However, as we have seen, at one highly significant point this line of continuity was ostensibly interrupted. In the 1920s and early 1930s, in keeping with the realist maxim, the beginnings of European integration or of a European Union were rejected as being against American interests and countered with the help of America's strategic partner, Germany; by contrast, beginning in 1947–48, the American government pursued the innovative policy of encouraging West European integration. In principle this policy has been retained to this day, although always with an important proviso—namely, *if* and *as long as* a nascent Europe pursues pro-American policies and does not exclude the United States from the decision-making process. Inasmuch as West European integration—above all as envisaged by the French—marked the start of the formation of a counterpoise to the United States, and if it was pursued in this way, it met with American resistance and prompted a change of course in the direction of the earlier anti-integrationist policy, wholly in keeping with the maxim that it was imperative to prevent a European concentration of power directed against the United States.

The reference to U.S. support for an integrative and federal peaceful order in Western Europe with a pro-American orientation points to another line of the continuity, and this must now be described somewhat more precisely on the basis of the historical analysis. It is the policy of universal order, the worldwide implementation of democracy and market economy in a multilateral and open international system without blocs and discrimination. This idealist policy was not—as is often assumed to be the case—in direct contrast to the realist policy of preventing hegemony or bloc formation in Europe. In fact, the formation of a European bloc stood in the way of global unity. In a way the universalist and idealist maxim and the realist maxim were and are two sides of the same coin, the pursuit of which defines the continuity of American policy on Europe in the twentieth century.

As we have seen, victory over the hegemonic challenger always occurred the moment when the policy of universal order came into its own. Here again there is a long line of continuity—from Wilson's "the world must be made safe for democracy" via Roosevelt's "one world" to Bush's "new world order" and Clinton's "engagement and enlargement." That the United States, as the strongest power, could develop best of all in an order of this kind was and is obvious, and is also the officially given reason for that policy. American leadership in the establishment and management of a democratic world community was and continues to be openly emphasized (and when, in the case of concrete attempts to put this into practice, as with the League of Nations, American decision-making freedom seemed restricted, the United States refused to participate).[207] What Americans tended to admit less frequently was that from the point of view of the other states, and also from the point of view of the West Europeans, American leadership meant "hegemony"—that is, not domination, but decisive influence;[208] and at the extreme, leadership together with other great powers ("partnership in leadership") or collective hegemony.[209]

Whenever this concept of order could not be implemented on a global scale (for example, after the First and Second World Wars, for partly similar and partly different reasons), the universalist concept of order and American leadership was reduced to Western Europe and transatlantic relations. Thus in the 1920s the United States laid the foundations for "economic peace" in Europe—as the leading economic power with the function of arbiter and balancer. After 1947–48 it laid the foundations for transatlantic and European peace—as the leading economic and military power with a hegemonic function, as balancer of the internal relationship of the European states, and as balancer against the Soviet empire, on both occasions with a strong involvement of social actors (transnational politics). The fact that on the second occasion there was institutionalization, and the creation of a formal alliance in peacetime, makes a profound difference. However, it is not that grave if we remember that, as in the case of the two preceding transatlantic coalitions, NATO was in real terms a wartime alliance, an alliance in the Cold War.

The length of the East-West conflict, the different ways it was dealt with, and above all the gradual increase in the power of European states and the decline in American economic power created differentiations of interest and modifications in American transatlantic hegemony, leading to symmetrical structures and the beginnings of collective leadership in the Atlantic alliance. It should be obvious that since the end of the East-West conflict, the three kinds of power shifts mentioned above have reinforced the symmetries in the transatlantic relationship. The consequences of this are difficult to predict. Nevertheless, the continuities outlined above permit us to make certain conjectures about what is likely to happen in the future.

Consequences for the Present and the Future

If it is correct that the continuities revealed in the historical analysis are of a long-term kind, then they can be expected to remain effective now and in the future, especially since there are not likely to be dramatic discontinuities.

Turning first to the United States, Presidents Bush and Clinton and influential groups and individuals have repeatedly spelled out universalist ideas of order. Furthermore, the realist maxim that it is necessary to prevent European or Eurasian hegemony after the end of the East-West conflict has been restated just as frequently. In the light of historical experience, it is hardly surprising that there is a fear of a new potential hegemonic threat from Russia and also from Germany and Japan.[210]

Of greater interest (and of greater importance for our concluding remarks) is that with the restatement both of the universalist and of the anti-hegemonic maxims, support for European integration or the EU tends to be seen in a critical light—not in public and official pronouncements, but in influential foreign policy analyses and diplomatic comments. This has been most clearly expressed by the American political scientist Samuel Huntington: "The political integration of the European Community, if that should occur, would also bring into existence an extraordinarily powerful entity which could not help but be perceived as a major threat to American interests." For this reason he believes that it is in American interests "to promote the evolution of the European Community in the direction of a looser, purely economic entity with broader membership rather than a tighter political entity with an integrated foreign policy."[211] The Bush administration concurred with this when it objected to the Franco-German initiative to turn the WEU into the defense arm of the EU, and Eurocorps into the core of an independent European military structure. In the administration's diplomatic initiative of February 21, 1991, the prospect of strengthening the "transatlantic partnership on security affairs with a more confident and united Europe" was welcomed, but it was followed by a direct and open warning: "In our view, efforts to construct a European pillar by redefining and delimiting NATO's role, by weakening its structure, or by creating a monolithic bloc of certain members would be misguided. We would hope such efforts would be resisted firmly."[212] Shortly afterward, the first version of the Pentagon's *Defense Planning Guidance for Fiscal Years 1994 to 1999* stated: "While the United States supports the goal of European integration, we must seek to prevent the emergence of European-only security arrangements which would undermine NATO, particularly the Alliance's integrated command structure."[213] In general terms it was also suggested that the challenge to American leadership by the great industrial states should be discouraged.[214]

President Clinton has emphasized a more positive attitude to the future development of the EU, although again with reference to the need for cooperation and the political maxim of open markets.[215] On the other hand, the West European governments have repeatedly stated that NATO continues to have priority in defense and security policy, and that a European defense organization should be established only if the United States is not able or willing to become involved in military terms.[216] As a consequence, compromise arrangements are typical of the current transitional period.

In the area of security policy, the agreement (persistently pursued by Germany) between France, Germany, and NATO concluded in December 1992 and January 1993 has disposed of the obvious irritations concerning Eurocorps. Thus the units assigned to Eurocorps (including the French ones) may under certain circumstances be placed under the control of NATO in the event of hostilities and for peacekeeping purposes.[217] The NATO agreement on developing capabilities for both WEU and NATO missions on the basis of the "separable but not separate" principle that was reached at the January 1994 summit foreshadows the future complementary structure.[218] In any case, a duplication of military capabilities would be impossible to implement because of the high costs of such a policy.[219]

However, as is shown by the Bosnian conflict, the practical political relevance of this agreement on military structures should not be overestimated. Neither the EU nor NATO has been able to prevent the war from escalating. And the tentative complementarity between EU/WEU and NATO is more a case of helplessness than of problem solving. The differences of opinion have led to polarization between the United States and Europe, and also to unconventional groupings (and here the shift in French policy in favor of greater American involvement is especially noteworthy).[220] As it turned out, NATO, not the EU or WEU, became the decisive actor. Within the alliance the transatlantic consensus to operate "out of area" on the basis of a U.N. mandate is perhaps the most important aspect.

In the area of trade policy the sharply divergent transatlantic interests and conflicts (in which the United States once more attempted to use the influence of Germany within the EU) were settled with a compromise reached at the GATT round, linking it to the important political decision to transform GATT into a world trade organization.[221]

Since the Transatlantic Declaration in November 1990, the EC/EU and the United States have with some success conducted a dialogue and engaged in mutual and regular consultations in important policy areas. The Common Foreign and Security Policy that the EU has attempted to pursue since the Maastricht Treaty could be integrated into similar dialogues. (Groups of experts are currently engaged in formulating suggestions for a common Euro-American policy of stabilization in Central and Eastern Europe.[222])

Finally, the policy of coordination pursued by the most important European and North American economic powers (together with the EU Commission) and Japan is being continued, and Russia is to some extent being drawn into the G-7 collective leadership. In the field of security policy the transatlantic alliance has organized cooperation with Central and East European states and with the Soviet Union's successor states below the level of NATO membership (North Atlantic Cooperation Council, Agreements on Partnership for Peace). This compromise makes it possible to differentiate between the security needs of the Central and East European states and the position of Russia, although without resolving the differences of opinion within the Atlantic alliance about the security policy organization of this geographic area. The discussion about NATO membership of these states is a case in point.

How should we interpret and assess these compromises in light of future transatlantic relations (and the relationship with Russia)? Do they represent the start of a symmetrical restructuring of the transatlantic relationship (and of a cooperative relationship between America, Europe, and Russia)? And is this the pattern of future developments?

The ambivalence both of the American policy on Europe and of the European states' "policy of Europeanization" is unmistakable. With regard to the future, the historical analysis provides an insight into the problem, and this may be summarized as follows.

A symmetrical transatlantic relationship—with the EU as independent actor—can be combined with the universalist maxim that it is imperative to prevent the formation of a European bloc only if Europe, in the process of unification, corresponds to American ideas of order and pursues a policy of open global trade and of peace; if the EU pursues a policy of open global trade and of peace; if the EU pursues a policy of cooperation that takes American interests into account; and if both sides regard mutual influence as legitimate and behave accordingly (even in those cases in which the United States uses its military presence in Europe to demonstrate its power outside Europe).

However, if the United States were to attempt to restore its former decisive leadership (hegemony) over Europe and to discourage the establishment of an independent European foreign policy, this would probably be counterproductive for the future of the transatlantic alliance. In all probability it would lead to the formation of a European counterpoise and to what Jeffrey Garten has called an economic "struggle for supremacy."[223]

If one assumes the continuity of the two American maxims and of Europe's will to assert itself (which is being demonstrated by the EU treaty), then a symmetrical and balanced transatlantic relationship would seem entirely appropriate. It would be particularly suited to neutralizing the potential or real hegemonic effect of American universalism and European unity. With the emergence of a symmetrical transatlantic structure of this kind the process of adjustment of the last three decades would reach its stated goal. What, under the constraints of the East-West conflict, could be implemented only in part or not at all because of Western Europe's dependence on American protection against the Soviet threat could now become a reality—in the interests of both sides.

However, structural change also implies discontinuity—with consequences for the functions that are the result of specific structures and that change those structures. American hegemony would become obsolete in a partnership between an integrated Europe and the United States, as would the internal balancer function within the alliance (especially with regard to Germany) or, alternatively, the use of Germany as a factor of strategic influence and as a continental European "vassal" of the United States (these functions, as we have seen, have been important elements of continuity in American policy on Europe since the interwar period and the end of the Second World War).

However, numerous influential commentators in the United States (and in Europe)[224] wish to adhere to these functions: the United States as "balancer and guarantor," as "geopolitical equalizer and benign arbiter," as a purveyor of "reassurance" against a German misuse of power, including a "strategic German-American partnership" in the stabilization of Central and Eastern Europe.[225] This is a clear sign that it cannot be generally assumed that there is readiness for structural change in the Atlantic alliance. One line of continuity is at variance with the other, and it will be necessary to choose between them or to try out a combination of the two; this is probably appropriate for the transitional period.

The decisive factor may well be whether the European states in fact wish to (and will) turn the EU into an independent entity, which is a precondition for a new balanced transatlantic partnership. European integration—after the ratification of the Maastricht Treaty—stands between federal integration and intergovernmental cooperation. To put it more precisely, in the EU both principles are specifically combined (with additional elements of a cooperative balance of power).[226] Given that there is no such thing as irreversibility in history, events may progress in one of two directions: back to a mere economic union in the sense of a large free trade area and political renationalization, or toward a political union (even if it involves "graded integration" or a *géometrie variable*).

In the case of the former there might be a resurgence of old European rivalries, the way "back to the future" that has been mapped out by the American political scientist John Mearsheimer.[227] The United States will then be forced to act as a balancer between the European great powers, either *against* Germany in order to prevent German hegemony or a German sphere of influence in Central and Eastern Europe, or *with* Germany to enable America to influence the policies of the European states (as in the 1920s and after the Second World War). And if the United States is unwilling to play the role of balancer, then the all-too-familiar circle of fear of hegemony and encirclement that has always been part of European history could recur, possibly leading to an antagonistic balance of power or even to a new war.

In the case of the latter (that is, political union) there would be a cooperative integration of German power through mutual control and restraint in accordance with the federal and confederal principle of integration. Max Kohnstamm, a former member of the EC Commission, has summed this up rather well by saying that Europe would "definitely bid good-bye to the twin concept of hegemony and balance of power."[228] And this would obviate the necessity for balance from overseas.

It has been demonstrated elsewhere that in the various European countries, the different interpretations of the American balancing function tend to be correlated with the differing assessments of the future of European integration, and that basically it is a matter of finding different solutions for the same problem: the prevention of renewed German hegemony or of a hegemonic policy.[229] The continuity of the American realist maxim suggests that on this fundamental point a common transatlantic interest will persist. It is difficult to imagine that Germany—which in the minds of its citizens is far from any kind of striving for hegemony, and whose politics are determined by a "culture of restraint"—could approve of a transatlantic alliance that sees its raison d'être largely in balancing German power and a potential Germany striving for hegemony. The same is doubtless true of the majority of Americans.[230] Furthermore, from an American point of view there is probably a significant difference between a federal or confederal Europe (with an integrated Germany) and a non-integrated and resurgent Germany as partner and counterpart in the transatlantic relationship.[231] It is obviously in the best interests of both Europe and America not to relinquish the innovation of European integration, and to continue to pursue and support further moves toward the political unification of Europe. Whether this line of continuity will persist is a fateful question for transatlantic cooperative relations.

If the transatlantic relationship—parallel to the rise of Europe as a political actor—were freed from the necessity to contain and balance Germany, it would be possible to formulate a common transatlantic response to the challenges of both the present and the future in the two "areas of crisis" in the east and south of Europe. For this a "new U.S.-European strategic bargain" would become necessary.[232]

In the past, the common threat and the value community formed the basis for the establishment of transatlantic coalitions and alliances. It remains to be seen whether the new challenges will have a unifying effect capable of providing a reason for the alliance that is similar to the response to the three great threats in the past. Some analysts of the current situation are even of the opinion that a unifying threat is not necessary for the continuation of the existing alliance, believing that the transatlantic community has acquired a life and a dynamic of its own. Despite antithetical comments and tendencies on both sides of the Atlantic, neither Americans nor Europeans are interested in an American withdrawal from Europe (that is, no "go-go scenario").[233] If this is true, then the time would seem ripe to embark in a cautious and stepwise manner on a restructuring of the transatlantic relationship so that it would correspond to the new distribution of power and to the challenges that lie ahead.

However, transformation does not come about of its own accord: it requires political action based on specifically defined interests. In Europe it is primarily France that, in a continuation of similar attempts in the 1920s and over the past four decades, is striving to achieve a symmetrical and balanced Euro-American relationship (and a European partnership with Japan and Russia), "l'emergence d'une politique de securité commune et une nouvelle relation d'alliance équilibrées avec les Etats-Unis."[234] In the long term even the *force de frappe* could become part of a European defense system through the formulation of a European nuclear doctrine.[235] That this policy is not directed against the continuation of the Atlantic alliance, and in fact wishes to ensure its existence, has been emphasized not only in rhetorical terms by the new neo-Gaullist government. Rather, everyday political practice in recent years has seen a "stealthy return of France to the various NATO committees."[236] Here the key phrase is "balance of interdependencies"—that is, "we accept a certain American influence on Europe in order to be able to exercise an influence on American policies."[237]

This goal coincides with German interests. It stands in the continuity of German foreign policy since Adenauer and has become of essential importance since reunification. Furthermore, on this subject there is a broad consensus among the political and societal elites and the German population as a whole. It explains why Germany and France are actively pursuing this policy with joint initiatives by Kohl and Mitterrand that aim to encourage European self-assertion and independence through integration, and that envisage a European Union that is an equal partner of America and dedicated to cooperation. Thus the visible elimination of

French political undercurrents directed against America or NATO has led to an even greater measure of Franco-German agreement.[238] As we have seen, the United States, given a pro-American or pro-Atlanticist tendency in the EU, would probably be prepared, in the context of its innovative postwar policy, to continue to pursue a pro-European approach. And here the intersocietal and transnational relationships (as in the past) will play an important role.[239]

To sum up, the stepwise restructuring of transatlantic relations on the lines of a symmetrical and balanced alliance (coupled with greater cooperation with Russia) is not inevitable, and there are alternatives. But it is a realistic vision capable of realization.[240] And it provides an opportunity to combine continuity and change in the Euro-Atlantic area in a constructive manner.[241]

NOTES

1. Alexander Gerschenkron, "On the Concept of Continuity in History," *Proceedings of the American Philosophical Society*, vol. 103 (1962), pp. 195–209. See also George Liska, "Continuity and Change in International Systems," *World Politics*, vol. 16 (1963–64), pp. 118–136. For an earlier study that makes use of these concepts, see Werner Link, "Zum Problem der Kontinuität der amerikanischen Deutschlandpolitik im zwanzigsten Jahrhundert," in M. Knapp, ed., *Die deutsch-amerikanischen Beziehungen nach 1945* (Frankfurt and New York: Campus Verlag 1975), pp. 86–131. See also Erhard Forndran, *Die Vereinigten Staaten von Amerika und Europa* (Baden-Baden: Nomos Verlag, 1991); and Hans-Jürgen Schröder, "Amerika als Modell. Die neue Weltordnung in historischer Perspektive," *Europa-Archiv* (1992), pp. 115–24. (*Europa-Archiv* is hereafter cited as *EA*.)
2. Kenneth N. Waltz, *Theory of International Politics* (Reading, Massachusetts: Addison-Wesley, 1979), p. 65.
3. Friedrich Meinecke, *Die Idee der Staatsräson in der neueren Geschichte*, 3rd ed. (Munich: R. Oldenbourg Verlag, 1963).
4. Waltz, *Theory of International Politics* (esp. ch. 6).
5. Nicholas J. Spykman, *America's Strategy in World Politics* (New York: Harcourt, Brace and Company, 1942). See also Werner Link, *Der Ost-West-Konflikt: Die Organisation der internationalen Beziehungen im 20. Jahrhundert*, 2nd ed. (Stuttgart: Kohlhammer, 1988), pp. 16 ff. The English edition, *The East-West Conflict* (Leamington Spa: Berg Publishers, 1986), does not contain the theoretical chapter that is of relevance in this context.

6. On the combination of transnational and neorealist approaches, see Werner Link, "Reflections on Paradigmatic Complementarity in the Study of International Relations," in E. O. Czempiel and J. N. Rosenau, eds., *Global Changes and Theoretical Challenges* (Lexington, Massachusetts: Lexington Books, 1989), pp. 99–116.
7. Ludwig Dehio, *Gleichgewicht oder Hegemonie: Betrachtungen über ein Grundproblem der neueren Staatengeschichte*, 3rd ed. (Krefeld: Scherpe Verlag n.d.). The term "hegemony" is used in the sense defined in Heinrich Triepel, *Die Hegemonie*, 2nd ed. (1943; reprint ed., Aalen: Scientia Verlag, 1974). Hegemony, in contrast to domination is taken to denote "control" and "prevailing and decisive influence" that is based on its acceptance and consent by the subordinate states.
8. It is, of course, imperative to avoid what the American Scholar David Hackett Fischer has called "fallacies of false analogy." Such traps have been described quite clearly in the literature, for "any intelligent use of analogy must begin with a sense of its limits," and differences are just as important as similarities. As Fischer says, a historical analysis of the continuities and discontinuities in transatlantic relations can and ought to "clarify contexts in which contemporary problems exist." It should not be used to predict a recurrence of the past under comparable or similar conditions. Rather, in the case of similar situations, constellations, and problems, it should point out the choice of options and alternative scenarios that continues to be the task of concrete political decision-making. See David Hackett Fischer, *Historians' Fallacies* (New York and Evanston, Illinois: Harper and Row Publishers, 1970), pp. 258 and 315.
9. John Winthrop, *A Model of Christian Charity*, cited in S. E. Morison, *The Oxford History of the American People* (New York: Oxford University Press, 1965), p. 65.
10. Washington's Farewell Address, cited in H. S. Commager, ed., *Documents of American History*, 7th ed. (New York: Appleton-Century-Crofts, 1962), vol. 1, pp. 169 ff.
11. Bernhard Fabian, *Alexis de Tocquevilles Amerikabild* (Heidelberg: C. Winter Verlag, 1957), p. 90.
12. Manfred Henningsen, *Der Fall Amerika* (Munich: List Verlag, 1974). The following remarks are based on this informative book, which also provides data on the subject of emigration.
13. Cited in Geoffrey Barraclough, "Europa, Amerika und Rußland in Vorstellung und Denken des 19. Jahrhunderts," *Historische Zeitschrift*, no. 203 (1966), p. 288.
14. Alexis de Tocqueville, *Democracy in America*, vol. 1 (New York: Alfred A. Knopf, 1940), pp. 13–14.
15. Günter Moltmann, *Atlantische Blockpolitik im 19. Jahrhundert* (Düsseldorf: Droste Verlag, 1973).

16. A statement made by the Italian revolutionary Mazzini cited in Barraclough, "Europa, Amerika und Rußland," p. 289. In the United States those in favor of American intervention in support of the liberal revolutionaries in Europe accused their political opponents of "isolationism." It was the origin of the battle cry of the interventionists, which has been used ever since. However, as the American historian Albert K. Weinberg has shown, it is of no use whatsoever in terms of political science analysis ("it indicates the misunderstanding of ideology"). For this reason it is not employed in the present study. See Albert K. Weinberg, "The Historical Meaning of the American Doctrine of Isolation," *American Political Science Review*, vol. 34 (1940), pp. 539–47.
17. De Tocqueville, *Democracy in America*, p. 428–29.
18. Ibid., p. 434.
19. Cited in Barraclough, "Europa, Amerika und Rußland," p. 303.
20. For example, see the remarks of Alexander Hill Everett in Fabian, *Alexis de Tocquevilles Amerikabild*, pp. 101 ff.
21. See Barraclough, "Europa, Amerika und Rußland"; and Heinz Gollwitzer, *Geschichte des weltpolitischen Denkens*. Vol. 2: *Zeitalter des Imperialismus und der Weltkriege* (Göttingen: Vandenhoeck and Ruprecht, 1982).
22. Fritz Fischer, *Griff nach der Welsmacht* (Dusseldorf: Drosle Verlag, 1961).
23. See Paul Kennedy, *The Rise and Fall of the Great Powers* (New York: Random House, 1987); and Walter LaFeber, "The 'Lion in the Path': The U.S. Emergence as a World Power," *Political Science Quarterly*, vol. 101 (1986), pp. 707–18.
24. Frank Costigliola, *Awkward Dominion: American Political, Economic, and Cultural Relations with Europe, 1919–1933* (Ithaca: Cornell University Press, 1984). "Factory on a Hill" is the title of the chapter about U.S. economic relations with Europe.
25. Cited in Emily S. Rosenberg, *Spreading the American Dream: American Economic and Cultural Expansion* (New York: Hill and Wang, 1982), p. 15.
26. Ibid., p. 22, citing J. G. Kitchell, *American Supremacy* (1901).
27. Ibid., pp. 50 f.
28. See Gollwitzer, *Geschichte des weltpolitischen Denkens*, vol. 2, pp. 149–95.
29. Cited in Rosenberg, *Spreading the American Dream*, p. 59.
30. A remark made by Andrew Barnaby after his journey to America in 1759–60, cited in Barraclough, "Europa, Amerika und Rußland," p. 284, n. 10.
31. See Rosenberg, *Spreading the American Dream*, pp. 15 ff. See also the numerous studies by William A. Williams and his pupils, and the comprehensive overview provided in Gollwitzer, *Geschichte des weltpolitischen Denkens*, vol. 2, pp. 256 ff.
32. See also the texts reproduced in Norman A. Graebner, ed., *Ideas and Diplomacy* (New York: Oxford University Press, 1964), ch. 7.
33. See Reiner Pommerin, *Der Kaiser und Amerika* (Cologne and Vienna: Böhlau Verlag, 1986).

34. Alfred Vagts, *Deutschland und die Vereinigten Staaten in der Weltpolitik* (New York and London: Lora, Dickson and Thompson, 1935).
35. See Pommerin, *Der Kaiser und Amerika*, ch. 2, which has the appropriate title "Vereinigte Staaten von Europa versus Vereingte Staaten von Amerika?"
36. Ibid., p. 293.
37. See Georges-Henri Soutou, *L'Or et le Sang: Les Buts de Guerre Economiques de la Première Guerre Mondiale* (Paris: Fayard, 1989).
38. David Calleo, "Deutschland und Amerika," in D. P. Calleo, R. Morgan, R. Poidevin, and M. Voslensky, eds., *Geteiltes Land—Halbes Land*? (Frankfurt and Berlin: Ullstein Verlag, 1986), pp. 54 f. See also Ragnhild Fiebig-von Hase, "The United States and Germany in the World Arena: 1900–1917," in H.-J. Schröder, ed., *Confrontation and Cooperation: Germany and the United States in the Era of World War I, 1900–1924* (Providence, Rhode Island, and Oxford: Berg Publishers, 1993), pp. 33–68.
39. Pommerin, *Der Kaiser und Amerika*, pp. 304 ff., describes this in greater detail.
40. Vagts, *Deutschland und die Vereinigten Staaten in der Weltpolitik*, pp. 1915 f.
41. See Reiner Pommerin, "Zum Interesse der USA am Erhalt der 'Balance of Power' in Europa im Zeitalter des Imperialismus," *Amerikastudien*, vol. 31 (1987), pp. 469–74. A case in point is an essay cleared for publication by the State Department, David L. Emstein, "The United States and Anglo-German Rivalry," *The National Review*, January 1913, pp. 736–50, parts of which have been reprinted in Paul Seabury, ed., *Balance of Power* (San Francisco: Chandler Publishers, 1965), pp. 68–74, and in Graebner, *Ideas and Diplomacy*, pp. 428 ff.
42. Wilson to his friend and adviser E. Dodd, August 15, 1915, cited in DeWitt C. Poole, "Balance of Power," *Life*, September 22, 1947, pp. 76–94; reprinted in Seabury, *Balance of Power*, pp. 126 f.
43. U.S. Ambassador David Francis, Petrograd, to President Wilson, February 22, 1917, cited in Lloyd C. Gardner, *Safe for Democracy* (Oxford: Oxford University Press, 1987), pp. 124 f.
44. See Link, *The East-West Conflict*, pp. 16–17, 61 ff.
45. See William A. Williams, *American-Russian Relations: 1781–1947* (New York and Toronto: Rimehart, 1952), and ———, *The Tragedy of American Diplomacy*, rev. ed. (New York: Dell Publishing, 1959). See also Arno J. Mayer, *Political Origins of the New Diplomacy: 1917–1918* (New Haven: Yale University Press, 1959); ———, *Politics and Diplomacy of Peacemaking* (New York: Alfred A. Knopf, 1967); and N. Gordon Levin, Jr., *Woodrow Wilson and World Politics* (New York: Oxford University Press, 1968).
46. Levin, *Woodrow Wilson and World Politics*, pp. 112 f. See also George F. Kennan, "The United States and the Soviet Union: 1917–1976," *Foreign Affairs*, vol. 54 (1976), pp. 670 ff.

47. See Mayer, *Politics and Diplomacy*; and John M. Thompson, *Russia, Bolshevism, and the Versailles Peace* (Princeton: Princeton University Press, 1967).
48. Gottfried Niedhart, "Zwischen Feindbild und Wunschbild: Die Sowjetunion in der britischen Urteilsbildung, 1917–1945," in G. Niedhart, ed. *Der Westen und die Sowjetunion* (Paderborn: Schöningh, 1983), pp. 106 f.
49. Cited in Costigliola, *Awkward Dominion*, p. 39.
50. Levin, *Woodrow Wilson and World Politics*, p. 191.
51. Cited in Klaus Schwabe, *Deutsche Revolution und Wilson-Frieden* (Düsseldorf: Droste Verlag, 1971), p. 117. Retranslation.
52. Cited in Levin, *Woodrow Wilson and World Politics*, p. 216.
53. Senator Henry Cabot Lodge on April 18, 1921, in a letter to Ellisloving Dresel, the American chargé d'affaires in Berlin. Dresel Papers (Houghton Library, Harvard University).
54. Niedhart, "Zwischen Feindbild und Wunschbild," p. 107.
55. On this and on the alternative, close Atlanticist ties with the West, see Werner Link, "Amerika, die Weimarer Republik und Sowjetrußland" in Niedhart, *Der Westen und die Sowjetunion*, pp. 79–104.
56. Klaus Hildebrand, *Das Deutsche Reich und die Sowjetunion im internationalen System: 1918–1932* (Wiesbaden: Steimer Verlag, 1977), p. 39.
57. A lucid survey is provided in Horst Günter Linke, "Deutschland und die Sowjetunion von Brest-Litowsk bis Rapallo," *Aus Politik und Zeitgeschichte*, April 15, 1972, pp. 23–38. On the "Rapallo complex," which has existed ever since, see Eberhard Kolb, *Die Weimarer Republik* (Munich and Vienna: Oldenbourg Verlag, 1984), pp. 191 ff.
58. A view expressed by William R. Castle, the head of the Western European Desk in the State Department on March 2, 1921, in a letter to the American chargé d'affaires in Berlin, cited in Link, "Amerika, die Weimarer Republik und Sowjetrußland," pp. 86 f.
59. Ibid., p. 90.
60. Communication from Hoover to Secretary of State Charles E. Hughes, December 6, 1921, cited in ibid., p. 90.
61. Memorandum from E. D. Durand, head of the Russian Desk in the Department of Commerce, February 2, 1922, cited in Link, *The East-West Conflict*, p. 69.
62. For statistical information see Link, "Amerika, die Weimarer Republik und Sowjetrußland," pp. 99 ff.
63. Herbert Feis, *1933: Characters in Crisis* (Boston and Toronto: Little, Brown and Co., 1966), p. 311.
64. Gilbert Ziebura, *Weltwirtschaft und Weltpolitik: 1922/24–1931* (Frankfurt am Main: Suhramp Verlag, 1984). For statistical information on global industrial output and related matters, see Derek H. Aldcroft, *Die zwanziger Jahre* (Munich: Deutscher Taschenbuch Verlag, 1978), pp. 336 f. However,

the so-called London school is of the opinion that American power was "more potential than real" in the 1920s. See the works cited in Brian McKercher, "Reaching for the Brass Ring: Recent Historiography of Interwar American Foreign Relations," *Diplomatic History*, vol. 15 (1991), pp. 585 ff.

65. This is confirmed in the most recent biography, August Heckscher, *Woodrow Wilson* (New York: Scribner, 1991). See also the survey of the literature in Lawrence E. Gelfand, "Where Ideals Confront Self-Interest: Wilsonian Foreign Policy," *Diplomatic History*, vol. 18 (1994), pp. 125–33.
66. Cited in Gardner, *Safe for Democracy*, p. 2.
67. Cited in Rosenberg, *Spreading the American Dream*, p. 94.
68. Ibid.
69. This has been pointed out repeatedly by Lloyd E. Ambrosius. For example, see his *Woodrow Wilson and the American Diplomatic Tradition: The Treaty Fight in Perspective* (Cambridge: Cambridge University Press, 1987).
70. Mayer, *Politics and Diplomacy*, p. 275.
71. Michael J. Hogan, "The United States and the Problem of International Economic Control," *Pacific Historical Review*, vol. 44 (1975), p. 98.
72. Schwabe, *Deutsche Revolution und Wilson-Frieden*, p. 194.
73. On this and the following section see Ambrosius, *Woodrow Wilson*; and ———, "Wilson, the Republicans, and French Security after World War I," *Journal of American History*, vol. 59 (1972–73), pp. 341–52.
74. Speech in the Senate on December 18, 1918, cited in Ambrosius, "Wilson, the Republicans, and French Security after World War I," p. 348.
75. This is analyzed and described in greater detail in Werner Link, *Die amerikanische Stabilisierungspolitik in Deutschland: 1921–32* (Düsseldorf: Droste Verlag, 1970).
76. See Walter A. McDougall, *France's Rhineland Diplomacy, 1914–1924: The Last Bid for a Balance of Power in Europe* (Princeton: Princeton University Press, 1978); and Marc Trachtenberg, *Reparations in World Politics, France and European Economic Diplomacy: 1916–1923* (New York: Columbia University Press, 1980).
77. The debts that had accumulated during the war as a result of the mutual financial assistance of the Allied and associated powers amounted to about U.S. $26.5 billion (and were thus less than the German reparations, which were fixed at U.S. $33 billion). The United States was debt-free and the principal creditor, with claims totaling U.S. $12 billion. Britain owed the United States U.S. $4.7 billion, but was also owed U.S. $11.1 billion by other Allies. In the case of France, debts were twice as high as claims (U.S. $7 billion vs. U.S. $3.5 billion). See Aldcroft, *Die zwanziger Jahre*, pp. 112–14.
78. On these three points see Link, *Die amerikanische Stabilisierungspolitik in Deutschland*; and ———, "Die Vereinigten Staaten und der Ruhrkonflikt," in K. Schwabe, ed., *Die Ruhrkrise 1923* (Paderborn: Schöningh, 1984), pp. 39–51. On the final point see also the detailed analysis by Elisabeth Glaser-

Schmidt, "German and American Concepts to Restore a Liberal World Trading System after World War I," in Schröder, *Confrontation and Cooperation*, pp. 353–76.

79. Stephen A. Schuker, *The End of French Predominance in Europe* (Chapel Hill: University of North Carolina Press, 1976).
80. See Rosenberg, *Spreading the American Dream*, pp. 154 ff.
81. Letter from Vice President Charles G. Dawes to Sir Josiah Stamp, July 20, 1925, cited in Link, *Die amerikanische Stabilisierungspolitik in Deutschland*, pp. 387 f.
82. A phrase used by Briand in a conversation with the German ambassador in Paris, cited in Robert Gottwald, *Die deutsch-amerikanischen Beziehungen in der Ära Stresemann* (Berlin-Dahlem: Colloquim Verlag, 1965), p. 91.
83. A statement made by the British ambassador in Berlin in the course of talks held at the German Foreign Ministry on May 28, 1930, and June 5, 1930, cited in Walter Lipgens, "Europäische Einigungsidee 1923–1930 und Briands Europaplan im Urteil der deutschen Akten," *Historische Zeitschrift*, no. 203 (1966), p. 326.
84. Ibid., p. 329.
85. Stresemann in the ministerial meeting on April 27, 1928, cited in Link, *Die amerikanische Stabilisierungspolitik in Deutschland*, p. 353.
86. A statement by Undersecretary of State Köpke on May 30, 1930, cited in Lipgens, "Europäische Einigungsidee," p. 330.
87. On November 4, 1925, the German embassy in Washington reported that commentators in the United States were increasingly interpreting "Locarno as the start of a process that could lead to a union of European powers next to the United States of America, and perhaps against them." Cited in Link, *Die amerikanische Stabilisierungspolitik in Deutschland*, p. 348.
88. Significantly, Germany did not participate in the retaliatory measures that most European states adopted against renewed U.S. protectionist tariffs (Hawley-Smoot Tariff). See Joseph M. Jones, Jr., *Tariff Retaliation: Repercussions of the Hawley-Smoot Bill* (Philadelphia: University of Pennsylvania Press, 1934).
89. Conversations between Secretary of State Henry Stimson and President Hoover on June 11, 1931, and October 24, 1931, cited in Link, *Die amerikanische Stabilisierungspolitik in Deutschland*, pp. 301 and 311.
90. Michael J. Hogan, *Informal Entente: The Private Structure of Cooperation in Anglo-American Economic Diplomacy, 1918–1928* (Columbia, MO, and London: University of Missouri Press, 1977).
91. Stephen V. O. Clark, *Central Bank Cooperation: 1924–31* (New York: Federal Reserve Bank of New York, 1967).
92. See Hogan, *Informal Entente*, p. 220; and Brian McKercher, "Wealth, Power, and the New International Order: Britain and the American Challenge in the 1920s," *Diplomatic History*, vol. 12 (1988), p. 438.
93. McKercher, "Reaching for the Brass Ring," p. 586.

94. Gustav Schmidt, "Die Position und Rolle Deutschlands in regionalen und internationalen Strukturen von der Jahrhundertwende bis zur Welwirtschaftskrise," in J. Kocka, H-J. Puhle, and K. Tenfelde, eds., *Von der Arbeiterbewegung zum modernen Sozialstaat, Festschrift für Gerhard Ritter* (Munich: K. G. Sour Verlag, 1994), p. 647.
95. See Lester V. Chandler, *Benjamin Strong: Central Banker* (Washington, D.C.: Brookings Institution, 1958), p. 280.
96. Cited in Costigliola, *Awkward Dominion*, p. 212.
97. Owen D. Young to Gerard Swope (General Electric Co.), February 7, 1930, cited in Josephine Young Case and Everett Needham Case, *Owen D. Young and American Enterprise* (Boston: David R. Godine, 1982), p. 485.
98. See Ziebura, *Weltwirtschaft und Weltpolitik*.
99. See Barry Eichengreen, *Golden Fetters: The Gold Standard and the Great Depression, 1919–1939* (Oxford: Oxford University Press, 1992), ch. 2; and Kennedy, *The Rise and Fall of the Great Powers*, p. 283.
100. Andrew P. N. Erdmann, "Mining for the Corporatist Synthesis: Gold in American Foreign Economic Policy, 1931–1936," *Diplomatic History*, vol. 17 (1993), p. 194.
101. Klaus Hildebrand, *Das Dritte Reich*, 2nd ed. (Munich and Vienna: Oldenbourg Verlag, 1980), pp. 26 ff.
102. See Hans-Jürgen Schröder, *Deutschland und die Vereinigren Staaten* (Wiesbaden: Steiner Verlag, 1970): and "Das Dritte Reich und die USA," in M. Knapp, W. Link, H.-J. Schröder, and K. Schwabe, eds., *Die USA und Deutschland: 1918–1975* (Munich: Beck Verlag, 1978), pp. 107–52.
103. See Rosenberg, *Spreading the American Dream*.
104. See Erdmann, "Mining for the Corporatist Synthesis," p. 197 ff; cf. n. 24.
105. Cited in Schröder, "Das Dritte Reich und die USA," p. 130.
106. See Klaus Hildebrand, *Deutsche Außenpolitik: 1933–1945*, 5th ed. (Stuttgart: Kohlhammer Verlag, 1990).
107. Bernd-Jürgen Wendt, *Economic Appeasement* (Düsseldorf: Droste Verlag, 1971), esp. pp. 331 ff., 525 ff., and 564 ff. For recent literature on the subject see Wolfgang Mommsen and Lothar Kettenacker, eds., *The Fascist Challenge and the Policy of Appeasement* (London: George Allen and Unwin, 1985); and Arnold A. Offner, "Misperceptions and Reality: Roosevelt, Hitler, and the Search for a New Order in Europe," *Diplomatic History*, vol. 15 (1991), pp. 607–19.
108. Andreas Hillgruber, "Der Faktor Amerika in Hitlers Strategie 1938–1941," in Andreas Hillgruber, ed., *Deutsche Großmacht und Weltpolitik im 19. und 20. Jahrhundert* (Düsseldorf: Droste Verlag, 1977), pp. 197–222. For current research on this subject see Hildebrand, *Das Dritte Reich*, pp. 170 f.
109. Hildebrand, *Deutsche Außenpolitik*, p. 222.
110. See Thomas G. Paterson, "The Abortive American Loan to Russia and the Origins of the Cold War: 1943–1946," *Journal of American History*, vol. 56 (1969), pp. 70–92.

111. Leading American politicians were fully aware that this "policy of exclusion" would prompt the Soviet Union to take severe countermeasures. For example, see "Memorandum by the Acting Secretary of State (Acheson) to President Truman, 25 September 1945," in *Foreign Relations of the United States 1945*, ii, pp. 48–50. (*Foreign Relations of the United States* is hereafter cited as *FRUS*.) I have dealt with this and the following elsewhere, and refer the reader to my earlier publications. See Link, *The East-West Conflict*, pp. 58–60; and "Handlungsspielräume der USA in der Entstehung des Ost-West-Gegensatzes 1945–1950," *Aus Politik und Zeitgeschichte*, June 25, 1983, pp. 19–26.
112. "Briefing Book Paper, British Plan for a Western European Bloc, 28 June 1945," *FRUS 1945, Conference of Berlin* I, p. 259.
113. Ibid., p. 264. These are the concluding words of the recommendations referred to above.
114. Ibid., p. 263.
115. Discussed in greater detail in Werner Link, "Die amerikanische Deutschlandpolitik: 1945–1949," in W. Link, ed., *Die Deutschlandfrage und die Anfänge des Ost-West-Konflikts: 1945–1949. Studien zu Deutschland-frage*, vol. 7 (Berlin: Dunker und Humblat Verlag, 1984), pp. 7–23. See also John Gimbel, "Die Vereinigten Staaten, Frankreich und der amerikanische Vertragsentwurf zur Entmilitarisierung Deutschlands," *Vierteljahrshefte für Zeitgeschichte*, vol. 22 (1974), pp. 258–86.
116. *FRUS, 1947*, II, p. 247.
117. Truman wrote: "There was one pitfall I intended to avoid. We did not intend to pay . . . the reparations bill for Europe." See Harry S. Truman, *Memoirs* (Garden City, New York: Doubleday, 1955), p. 323. See also Robert Cecil, "Potsdam and Its Legends," *International Affairs*, vol. 46 (1970), p. 455 ff. On December 19, 1947, Secretary of State Marshall declared at the conference of foreign ministers in London that "reparations from current production—that is, export of day-to-day German production with no return—could be made only if the countries at present supplying Germany—notably the United States—foot the bill. We put in and the Russians take out." See Committee on Foreign Relations, U.S. Senate, *Documents on Germany: 1944–1961* (New York, 1968), p. 85.
118. See Henry L. Stimson and McGeorge Bundy, *On Active Service in Peace and War* (New York: Harper, 1948); Henry Stimson, "Memorandum for the President, 16 July 1945," *FRUS, The Conference of Berlin II*, pp. 754 ff.; Lucius D. Clay, *Entscheidung für Deutschland* (Frankfurt: Verlag der Frankfurte Heffe, n.d.); Wolfgang Krieger, *General Lucius Clay und die amerikanische Deutschlandpolitik: 1945–1949* (Stuttgart: Klett-Cotta, 1987); Robert Murphy, *Diplomat among Warriors* (New York: Collins, 1964); Walter Millis, ed., *The Forrestal Diaries* (New York: Viking, 1951); John Foster Dulles, "Europe Must Federate or Perish," *Vital Speeches of the*

Day, February 1, 1947, pp. 234 ff.; Alfred P. Sloan and Bernard M. Baruch, November 30, 1945 (reprinted in Walter Lafeber, *The Origins of the Cold War* [New York: John Wiley], 1967, pp. 129 ff.). See also Lloyd Gardner, *Architects of Illusion* (Chicago: Quadrangle Books, 1970). Among the opinion leaders, the *New York Times* began to advocate the policy of reintegration at an early stage. For example, an editorial on July 12, 1945, stated: "the pace of Europe's reconstruction . . . will depend to a large extent on the speed, the extent, and the purpose for which that economic heart (i.e., Germany) can be made to function" (p. 10).

119. See "Policy Statement on Reparations by the Department of State" and "Statement by the Secretary of State," in B. U. Ratchford and W. D. Ross, eds., *Berlin Reparations Assignment* (Chapel Hill: University of North Carolina Press, 1947), pp. 214 ff.
120. Ibid., p. 217.
121. Cited in Max Beloff, *The United States and the Unity of Europe* (London: Random House, 1963), p. 18.
122. On this and the following points see Walter Lipgens, *Die Anfänge der europäischen Einigungspolitik 1945–1950, part 1: 1945–1947* (Stuttgart: Klett Verlag, 1977). See also Gesine Schwan, "Europa as Dritte Kraft," in P. Haungs, ed., *Europäisierung Europas?* (Baden-Baden: Nomos Verlag, 1989), pp. 13–40.
123. For a more detailed discussion see Link, *The East-West Conflict,* chs. 7 and 8.
124. "Memorandum of Conversation," The White House, April 3, 1949 (a meeting attended by the president of the United States, the U.S. secretary of state, the U.S. secretary of defense, and the foreign ministers of the other NATO states on the eve of the signing of the NATO Treaty). Cited in Cees Wiebes and Bert Zeeman, "Eine Lehrstunde in Machtpolitik," *Vierteljahrsheft für Zeitgeschichte*, vol. 49 (1992), pp. 415–23. This key document—the editors are right to speak of "an object lesson in power politics"—also refutes the notion that the United States rejected the (European) balance-of-power concept. See also the published documents for 1948 and 1949, in *FRUS*, 1948 and 1949.
125. See Detlev Felken, *Dulles und Deutschland* (Bonn: Bouvier Verlag, 1993), p. 63.
126. Dulles, *Europe Must Federate*.
127. See Charles S. Maier and Günter Bischof, eds., *The Marshall Plan and Germany* (New York and Oxford: Berg Publishers, 1991). For an American view see Hadley Arkes, *Bureaucracy, the Marshall Plan, and the National Interest* (Princeton: Princeton University Press, 1972).
128. See above, n. 124. The following quotations come from the "Memorandum of Conversation." For a good survey of how NATO came into existence, see Con Cook, *Forging the Alliance: NATO, 1945–1950* (New York: Arbor

House, 1989). See also Timothy Ireland, *Creating the Entangling Alliance: The Origins of the North Atlantic Treaty Organization* (Westport, Connecticut: Greenwood Press, 1981).

129. On the origins of the Marshall Plan see John Gimbel, *The Origins of the Marshall Plan* (Stanford, California: Stanford University Press, 1976); and Raymond Poidevin, "Ambiguous Partnership: France, the Marshall Plan and the Problem of Germany," in Maier and Bischof, *The Marshall Plan and Germany*, p. 359.

130. Thomas Schwartz, *European Integration and the "Special Relationship": Implementing the Marshall Plan in the Federal Republic*, p. 201.

131. Reprinted in *Politique Etrangère*, vol. 58 (1993), pp. 121–25. See also Klaus Schwabe, ed., *Die Anfänge des Schuman-Plans: 1950/51* (Baden-Baden: Nomos Valley, 1988).

132. This was the phrase used by George Kennan in 1947 in connection with the Marshall Plan, cited in Steve Weber, "Shaping the Postwar Balance of Power: Multilateralism in NATO," *International Organization*, vol. 46 (1992), p. 645. On the diverging goals and the question of integration see Michael J. Hogan, "European Integration and German Reintegration: Marshall Planners and the Search for Recovery and Security in Western Europe," in Maier and Bischof, *The Marshall Plan and Germany*, pp. 156 ff.

133. See Werner Link, "Die Rolle der USA im westeuropäischen Integrationsprozeß," *Aus Politik und Zeitgeschichte*, April 1, 1972, pp. 3–13.

134. See Charles S. Maier, "The Two Postwar Eras and the Conditions for Stability in Twentieth-Century Western Europe," *American Historical Review*, vol. 86 (1981), p. 344; and Alan S. Mitward, "The Marshall Plan and German Foreign Trade," in Maier and Bischof, *The Marshall Plan and Germany*, pp. 453 f.

135. Robert O. Keohane, *After Hegemony* (Princeton: Princeton University Press, 1984), ch. 8.

136. Josef Joffe, "Europe's American Pacifier," *Foreign Policy*, vol. 54 (1984), pp. 64–82; and ———, *The Limited Partnership: Europe, the United States and the Burdens of Alliance* (Cambridge, Massachusetts: Ballinger, 1987).

137. See Karl W. Deutsch et al., *Political Community and the North Atlantic Area* (Princeton: Princeton University Press, 1957).

138. See Link, *The East-West Conflict*, pp. 115–117 and ch. 10.

139. Michael J. Hogan, "American Marshall Planners and the Search for a European Neo-Capitalism," *American Historical Review*, vol. 90 (1985), pp. 44–72.

140. See Werner Link, *Deutsche und amerikanische Gewerkschaften und Geschäftsleute: 1945–1975. Eine Studie über transnationale Beziehungen* (Düsseldorf: Droste Verlag, 1978); and ———, "Building Coalitions: Non-governmental German-American Linkages," in Maier and Bischof, *The Marshall Plan and Germany*, pp. 282–330.

141. See Lawrence B. Krause, *European Economic Integration and the United States* (Washington, D.C.: Brookings Institution, 1968).
142. Jean-Jacques Servan-Schreiber, *Die amerikanische Herausforderung (Le défi américain)* (Hamburg: Hoffmann und Campe Verlag, 1970).
143. On Gaullist policies see also Edward A. Kolodziej, *French International Policy under de Gaulle and Pompidou* (London: Cornell University Press, 1974).
144. De Gaulle's memorandum of September 17, 1958, is reprinted in Alfred Grosser, *Das Bündnis* (Munich: Hanser Verlag, 1982), p. 264.
145. See the documents published in *Akten zur Auswärtigen Politik der Bundesrepublik Deutschland 1963*, vol. 1 (Munich: Oldenbourg Verlag, 1993).
146. See Hans-Peter Schwarz, *Adenauer, der Staatsmann: 1952–1967* (Stuttgart: Deutsche Verlagsanstaft, 1991). See also Werner Link, "Adenauer, Amerika und die deutsche Nachwelt," in K. Schwebe, ed., *Adenauer und die USA* (Rhöndorfer Gespräche), vol. 14 (Bonn: Bouvier Verlag, 1994), pp. 130–50.
147. See Martin Saeter, *Europa politisch* (Berlin: Colloquium Verlag, 1974).
148. See the pro-Atlanticist declaration signed by 19 prominent German businessmen, labor leaders, and politicians that Lucius Clay released to the press on March 21, 1963, reprinted in *Die Welt*, March 22, 1963. See also Link, *Deutsche und amerikanische Gewerkschaften und Geschäftsleute*, pp. 231 f.
149. See the revealing documents published in *Akten zur Auswärtigen Politik der Bundesrepublik Deutschland, 1963 and 1964* (Munich: Oldenbourg Verlag, 1994 and 1995). Further volumes are forthcoming.
150. Christoph Hoppe, *Zwischen Teilhabe und Mitsprache: Die Nuklearfrage in der Allianzpolitik Deutschlands, 1959–1966* (Baden-Baden: Nomos Verlag, 1993).
151. See Helga Haftendorn, *Kernwaffen und die Glaubwürdigkeit der Allianz: Die NATO-Krise von 1966/67* (Baden-Baden: Nomos Verlag, 1994).
152. "Die künftigen Aufgaben der Allianz" (December 1967), in *NATO: Tatsachen und Dokumente* (Brussels, 1976), pp. 375 ff. See also Helga Haftendorn, "Entstehung und Bedeutung des Harmel-Berichtes der NATO von 1967," *Vierteljahreshefte für Zeitgeschichte*, vol. 40 (1992), pp. 169–221, and ch. 5.
153. See Werner Link, "Außen- und Deutschlandpolitik in der Ära Brandt: 1969–1979," in K. D. Bracher, W. Jaga and W. Link, eds., *Geschichte de Bundesrepublik Deutschland, vol. 5. no. 1: Republic in Lvandel, 1969–1979. Die Ara Brandt* (Stuttgart and Mannheim: Deutsche Verlaganstalt, 1986), pp. 179–241.
154. Ibid., pp. 171 ff.
155. Helga Haftendorn, *Kernwaffen und die Glaubwürdigkeit der Allianz*, pp. 367 f.
156. See Kennedy's speech of July 4, 1962, reprinted in *EA* (1962), pp. D373–76.
157. My argument is based on the critical assessment of the partnership concept outlined in Stanley Hoffmann, *Gulliver's Troubles oder die Zukunft des Internationalen Systems* (Düsseldorf: Bertelsmann Verlag, 1970), pp. 424 ff.

158. See Dieter Dettke, *Allianz im Wandel: Europäisch-amerikanische Sicherheitsbeziehungen in der Phase des Bilateralismus der Supermächte* (Frankfurt: Metzne Verlag, 1976); and Reinhardt Rummel, *Zusammengesetzte Außenpolitik: Westeuropa als internationaler Akteur* (Kehl and Strasbourg: N.P. Engel Verlag, 1982). The documents relating to EPC have been made available in Presse- und Informationsdienst der Bundesregierung, *Europäische Politische Zusammenarbeit (EPZ): Eine Dokumentation der Bundesregierung* (Bonn, 1974).
159. Kissinger's proposals are reprinted in *EA* (1973), pp. D220–25. See also Henry A. Kissinger, *Memoiren* (Munich: Bertelsmann Verlag, 1982), vol. 4, pp. 218 ff.
160. See "Text of the European Economic Community's Proposal on Relations with the U.S.," *New York Times*, September 24, 1973, p. 16. See also *EA* (1974), pp. 141 ff.
161. The main protagonists were Henry Kissinger (see the account given in his memoirs) and French Foreign Minister Michel Jobert. See the latter's memoirs, *L'autre regard* (Paris: Bernard Grasset, 1974).
162. *Archiv der Gegenwart*, March 15, 1974, pp. 18571 f.
163. On this see Link, *Außen- und Deutschlandpolitik in der Ära Brandt*, pp. 260 ff., the chapter entitled "Die Neuregelung des europäisch-amerikanischen Dialogs."
164. Ibid., pp. 264 f.
165. Reprinted in *EA* (1974), pp. D339–41.
166. C. Fred Bergsten, "Die amerikanische Europa-Politik angesichts der Stagnation des Gemeinsamen Marktes: Ein Plaidoyer für Konzentration auf die Bundesrepublik," *EA* (1974), pp. 115–22 (proceedings of a hearing of two subcommittees of the House of Representatives Committee on Foreign Relations, November 3, 1973).
167. See Robert D. Putnam and Nicholas Bayne, *Hanging Together: The Seven-Powers Summit* (London: Heimemann, 1984).
168. See Werner Link, "Die Außen- und Deutschlandpolitik in der Ära Schmidt: 1974–1982," in W. Jäger and W. Link, eds., *Geschichte der Bundesrepublik Deutschland. Volume 5, Number 2: Republik im Wandel, 1978–1982: Die Ära Schmidt* (Stuttgart und Mannheim: Deutsche 1987), pp. 286 ff.
169. Ibid., pp. 317 ff.
170. See Hubertus Hoffmann, *Die Atompartner: Washington-Bonn und die Modernisierung der taktischen Kernwaffen* (Koblenz: Bernard und Graeve Verlag, 1986).
171. See Helmut Schmidt, *Menschen und Mächte* (Berlin: Siedler Verlag, 1987), pp. 226 ff.; and Lothar Rühl, *Mittelstreckenwaffen in Europa* (Baden-Baden: Nomos Verlag, 1987). On the SALT II negotiations see also Strobe Talbott, *Endgame: The Inside Story of SALT II* (New York: Harper and Row, 1979).

172. See Hans-Jürgen Küsters, "Die außenpolitische Zusammenarbeit der Neun und die KSZE," in H. Haftendorn et al., eds., *Verwaltete Außenpolitik* (Cologne: Verlag Wissenschaft und Politik, 1978), pp. 85–98.
173. See John J. Maresca, *To Helsinki: The Conference on Security and Cooperation in Europe, 1973–1975* (Durham, North Carolina, and London: Duke University Press, 1985); Vojtech Mastny, *The Helsinki Process and the Reintegration of Europe: 1986–1991* (London: Pinter Publishers, 1992); and Ingo Peters, *Transatlantischer Konsens und Vertrauensbildung in Europa* (Baden-Baden: Nomos Verlag, 1987). Before 1989 the question of whether a new order for the whole of Europe should merely be a cooperative stabilization of East-West relations (with "more organic" relations between the Soviet Union and its allies), or whether the bloc system itself ought to be dissolved, continued to be a matter for debate on both sides of the Atlantic. The predominant orientation in the United States toward the continuation of the structural status quo was forcefully expressed in A. W. DePorte, *Europe between the Superpowers: The Enduring Balance*, 2nd ed. (New York and London: Yale University Press, 1986).
174. On the transition from détente to confrontation see Raymond Garthoff, *Détente and Confrontation* (Washington, D.C.: Brookings Institution, 1985); on the two phases in the 1980s see Link, *Der Ost-West-Konflikt*, pp. 203 ff. See also E.-O. Czempiel, *Die Machtprobe: Die USA und die Sowjetunion in den achtziger Jahren* (Munich: Beck Verlag, 1989).
175. The United States frequently overlooked the fact that the Europeans made a large contribution to the alliance (about 90 percent of the ground forces and 80 percent of the combat aircraft). See Bundesminister der Verteidigung, *Weißbuch 1979* (Bonn, 1979), p. 23.
176. See Forndran, *Die Vereinigten Staaten von Amerika und Europa*, pp. 196 ff.
177. On this and the following see Link, "Die Außen- und Deutschlandpolitik in der Ära Schmidt," pp. 321 ff.
178. See Forndran, *Die Vereinigten Staaten von Amerika und Europa*, pp. 223 ff.
179. See Link, "Die Außen- und Deutschlandpolitik in der Ära Schmidt," pp. 343 ff.
180. Wolfgang Schreiber, *Die Strategische Verteidigungsinitiative—Vorgeschichte, Konzeption, Perspektiven, Forschungsbericht der Konrad-Adenauer-Stiftung, Nr. 45* (Melle, 1985).
181. See Wolfram F. Hanrieder, *Germany, America, Europe* (New Haven, Connecticut, and London: Yale University Press, 1989), pp. 122 ff.
182. See Christian Hacke, *Weltmacht wider Willen: Die Außenpolitik der Bundesrepublik Deutschland*, 2nd ed. (Stuttgart: Ullstein Verlag, 1993), ch. 7.
183. See Colin S. Gray and Keith Payne, "Victory Is Possible," *Foreign Policy*, vol. 39 (1980), pp. 21 ff.; and Helga Haftendorn, "Historische Entwicklung, politische Motive und rechtliche Grundlagen," in D. Mahncke, ed., *Amerikaner in Deutschland* (Bonn: Bourier Verlag, 1991), pp. 167 f.

184. Helmut Schmidt, "Europa muß sich selbst behaupten," *Die Zeit*, November 21, 1986. See also Peter R. Weilemann, "Der Wandel in Westeuropa," in Mahncke, *Amerikaner in Deutschland*, pp. 53–97; and Peter Schmidt, "Amerikanische Präsenz und die Rolle Deutschlands in der Politik der westeuropäischen Verbündeten," ibid., pp. 279–97.
185. See Peter Schell, *Bündnis im Schatten: Die Westeuropäische Union in den 80er Jahren* (Bonn: Bouvier Verlag, 1991).
186. In February 1986 the EC countries became signatories to the Single European Act, which initiated the creation of a unified internal market by 1993.
187. See Karl Kaiser and Pierre Lellouche, eds., *Deutsch-französische Sicherheitspolitik* (Bonn: Europa Union Verlag, 1986). The establishment of the Franco-German Defence Council on the 25th anniversary of the signing of the Franco-German cooperation treaty on January 22, 1963 (the Elysée Treaty), marked an increase in the level of cooperation. See the documentation in *EA* (1988), pp. D131–32.
188. See Link, *Der Ost-West-Konflikt*, pp. 214 ff.
189. See Michael Broer, *Die nuklearen Kurzstreckenwaffen in Europa* (Frankfurt am Main: Peter Lang Verlag, 1993). See also K.-P. Stratmann, "Die Stationierung amerikanischer Streitkräfte in Europa," in Mahncke, *Amerikaner in Deutschland*, p. 364: and Forndran, *Die Vereinigten Staaten von Amerika und Europa*, pp. 248 ff.
190. Rüdiger Hartmann, Wolfgang Heydrich, and Nikolaus Meyer-Landrut, *Der Vertrag über konventionelle Streitkräfte in Europa* (Baden-Baden: Nomos Verlag, 1994).
191. Ibid., p. 18.
192. Karl Kaiser, *Deutschlands Vereinigung: Die internationalen Aspekte* (Bergisch-Gladbach: Bastei-Lübbe Verlag, 1991); Michael R. Beschloss and Strobe Talbott, *Auf höchster Ebene: Das Ende des Kalten Krieges und die Geheimdiplomatie der Supermächte 1989–1991* (Düsseldorf: Econ Verlag, 1993); and Anatoli Tschernajew, *Die letzten Jahre einer Weltmacht* (Stuttgart: Deutsche Verlags-Anstaft, 1993).
193. Reprinted in *EA* (1990), pp. 456–60. In this declaration, NATO promised to develop "a new strategy" and invited the member states of the Warsaw Pact to sign a joint statement, "to consider each other no longer as adversaries."
194. See, for instance, Margaret Thatcher, *Downing Street No. 10, Memoirs*, (Düsseldorf: Econ, 1993), pp. 1085, 1095, and 1127; and "Werner Link, Europäische Interessen and der Funktion der USA als europäische Balancemacht," in Uwe Nerlich and Wolfgang Heydrich, eds., *Internationales Umfeld, Sicherhuts-interessen und nationale Planung der Bundesrepublik* (Ebenhausen: Stiftung Wicsenschaft und Politik, 1993), pp. 169–99, esp. pp. 190 ff.
195. This idea is still occasionally aired by Russian policymakers. See Marc Fisher, "Germany Says Russia Seeks a Policy Ally," *International Herald Tribune*, February 3, 1993, cited in Kenneth N. Waltz, "The Emerging Structure of International Politics," *International Security*, vol. 18 (1993), p. 75.

196. Thomas Läufer, ed., *Europäische Gemeinschaft–Europäische Union: Die Vertragstexte von Maastricht* (Bonn: Europa Union Verlag, 1992); and Werner Weidenfeld, ed., *Maastricht in der Analyse* (Gütersloh: Bertelsmann Verlag, 1994).
197. See *EA* (1991), pp. D18–21. This made up for what had failed to materialize in 1973–1994 (see above). With regard to the implementation of this declaration of intent, see Reinhardt Rummel, *Der Dialog zwischen der Europäischen Union und den Vereinigten Staaten: Erfahrungen mit der Transatlantischen Erklärung und Fragen ihrer Weiterentwicklung* (Stiftung Wissenchaft und Politik, Ebenhausen, 1994).
198. The phrase used by President Bill Clinton in his report, *A National Security Strategy of Engagement and Enlargement*, which was presented to the Congress on July 21, 1994. Reprinted in *Amerika Dienst*, July 27, 1994.

     Some adherents of the "realist" school (in contrast to those of the "decline" school) argue that only the United States possesses "imposing strength" in *all* the categories of power (thus the Clinton report states that "American assets are unique"), and that therefore the present international system is unipolar. However, under the rules of counterpoise formation that govern the conduct of emerging great powers, it will be transformed into a multipolar system. See Christopher Layne, "The Unipolar Illusion: Why New Great Powers Will Rise," *International Security*, vol. 17 (1993), pp. 3–51. See also Charles Krauthammer, "The Unipolar Illusion," *Foreign Affairs*, vol. 70 (1991), pp. 23–33. As to the present situation, even adherents of the interdependence school believe that "no country is at this time well positioned to challenge the United States for global leadership." See Joseph S. Nye, Jr., *Bound to Lead* (New York: Basic Books, 1990), p. 21.
199. Henry A. Kissinger, *Die Vernunft der Nationen* (Berlin: Siedler Verlag, 1994), p. 895.
200. See Richard Rosecrance, "A New Concert of Powers," *Foreign Affairs*, vol. 2 (1992), pp. 64–82; Charles A. Kupchan and Clifford A. Kupchan, "Concerts, Collective Security, and the Future of Europe," *International Security*, vol. 16 (1991), pp. 114–61; Robert Jervis, "The Future of World Politics," *International Security*, vol. 16 (1991), pp. 39–73; and Stanley Hoffmann, "Balance, Concert, Anarchy, or None of the Above," in G. F. Treverton, ed., *The Shape of the New Europe* (New York: Council on Foreign Relations Press, 1992), pp. 194–220.
201. See the remarks made by Secretary of State Warren Christopher to the Senate Foreign Relations Committee on November 4, 1993 (*Vital Speeches of the Day*, January 1, 1994, pp. 162–67), and his statement in *International Herald Tribune*, March 23, 1994: "President Clinton has placed America's economic strength at the heart of U.S. national security strategy in the post–Cold War world. The administration's foreign policy, like the country, stands for open societies as well as open markets. We are convinced that the two are insep-

arably linked." See also C. Fred Bergsten, "The Primacy of Economics," *Foreign Policy*, vol. 87 (1992), pp. 3–24. President Clinton's July 1994 report on national security strategy mentions three central goals: "To credibly sustain our security with military forces that are ready to fight. To bolster America's economic revitalization. To promote democracy abroad." Significantly this is followed by the remark "that we must revitalize our economy if we are to sustain our military forces, foreign initiatives and global influence, and that we must engage actively abroad if we are to open foreign markets and create jobs for our people."

202. Edward Luttwak, *The Endangered American Dream* (New York: Simon and Schuster, 1993).
203. This model was advocated in the 1960s by Bundestag President Eugen Gerstenmaier, *Streit und Friede hat seine Zeit* (Frankfurt am Main: Propyläen Verlag, 1981), p. 510. At the end of the 1980s, Karl Lamers, member of the German Bundestag (Christian Democratic Party), advocated it, for example, in a speech to the German Bundestag on December 7, 1989. See *Proceedings of the Deutsche Bundestag* (Bonn, 1989), p. 14021.
204. See Werner Link, "Kooperative Machtbalance und europäische Föderation als außenpolitische Orientierung," in W. Heydrich et al., eds., *Sicherheitspolitik Deutschlands* (Baden-Baden: Nomos Verlag, 1992), pp. 601–11. See also the other essays in that volume.
205. See Michael Smith and Stephen Woodcock, *The United States and the European Community in a Transformed World* (London: Pinter Publishers, 1993).
206. George Bush, "National Security Strategy of the United States" (New York: Brassey's, 1990), p. 5.
207. In the U.N. system the veto rights accorded to the permanent members of the Security Council protect the decision-making freedom of the great powers, and thus also that of the United States. A historical analysis demonstrates that this provision was the decisive precondition for U.S. membership. See Max Hagemann, *Der provisorische Frieden* (Erlenbach-Zurich and Stuttgart: E. Rentsch Verlag, 1964).
208. See Triepel, *Die Hegemonie*.
209. This was the original concept of the United Nations. See Robert C. Hilderbrand, *Dumbarton Oaks: The Origins of the United Nations and the Search for Postwar Security* (Chapel Hill: University of North Carolina Press, 1990).
210. For example, see President Bush's August 1991 "Report on National Security Strategy," in which the rise of Japan and Germany as economic and political leaders is considered "one of the most important and far-reaching strategic developments of a new era," and in which both states, despite their friendly relations with the United States, are described as "sometimes even

bitter competitors—in the economic arena." The possibility of German economic hegemony in Central and Eastern Europe has been examined in Andrei S. Markovits and Simon Reich, "Deutschlands neues Gesicht: Uber deutsche Hegemonie in Europa," *Leviathan*, vol. 20 (1992), pp. 15–63.

211. Samuel P. Huntington, "America's Changing Strategic Interests," *Survival*, vol. 33 (1991), pp. 12 f.
212. The text of this initiative has not been made public, although the author possesses a copy of it.
213. *Washington Post*, May 24, 1992.
214. See Josef Joffe, "Amerikas Große Strategie nach dem Kalten Kriege," in Heydrich et al., *Sicherheitspolitik Deutschlands*, pp. 109–23; and Klaus-Dieter Schwarz, "Die USA im Ubergang zur post-konfrontativen Weltordnung," ibid., pp. 87–107.
215. For example, at the NATO summit in Brussels in January 1994 and at the Euro-American summit in Berlin in July 1994. See *International Herald Tribune*, January 10, 1994; and Rummel, *Dialog* (the documents in the appendix are of special interest). The July 1994 report *A National Security Strategy of Engagement and Enlargement* states: "Our goal is an integrated democratic Europe cooperating with the United States to keep the peace and promote prosperity" (p. 36). The support of the EU is particularly mentioned with regard to U.S. wishes "to build on vibrant and open market economics" (p. 38).
216. This has been emphasized repeatedly by the German government.
217. See Andrew Denison, "Amerika und das Eurokorps," *Europäische Sicherheit*, vol. 3 (1993), ff. pp. 123–26.
218. Declaration of the Heads of State and Government, NATO Summit Meeting, Brussels, January 10–11, 1994, reported by Agence Europe, January 12, 1994.
219. According to a Rand study, the cost of an independent and comprehensive satellite surveillance and reconnaissance system would amount to about U.S. $46 billion over a period of 25 years. See Gebhard Schweigler. "The 'Go-Go-Scenario': The American Engagement in Europe," unpublished, May 1992, p. 4, n. 5.
220. See Gerd Koslowski, *Die NATO und der Krieg in Bosnien-Herzegowina* (Kölner Arbeiten Zur Internationalen Politik, vol. 2, Vierow: SH-Verlag, 1995). On the WEU see Luisa Vierucci, "WEU: A Regional Partner of the United Nations," *Chaillot Papers*, no. 12 (December 1993).
221. For example, see Bernhard May, *Die Uruguay-Runde* (Bonn: Europa Union Verlag, 1994).
222. See Rummel, *Dialog*.
223. See Jeffrey E. Garten, *A Cold Peace: America, Japan, Germany, and the Struggle for Supremacy* (New York: Times Books, 1992). From 1993–95, Jeffrey Garten was undersecretary of Commerce for international trade. He is now dean of the Yale School of Management,
224. See Link, "Europäische Interessen an der Funktion der USA als europäische Balancemacht."

225. Report of a group of politicians made up of leading security experts of both parties, *International Herald Tribune*, March 4, 1991. See also Daniel S. Hamilton, *Beyond Bonn: America and the Berlin Republic* (Washington, D.C.: Carnegie Endowment for International Peace, 1994), p. 22. Layne, "The Unipolar Illusion," also argues in favor of a U.S. balancer function in Europe (although without a military presence). Charles Mayne, "A Workable Clinton Doctrine," *Foreign Policy*, vol. 26 (Winter 1993–1994), p. 10, sees the future American security function as "balancer and conciliator rather than protector or guarantor."
226. See Werner Link, "Perpektiven der europäischen Integration," in K. Kaiser and H. W. Maull, eds., *Die Zukunft der europäischen Integration* (Bonn: Europa Union Verlag, 1993), pp. 7–26. See also Reinhardt Rummel, ed., *Toward Political Union* (Boulder: Nomos Verlag, 1992).
227. John J. Mearsheimer, "Back to the Future: Instability in Europe after the Cold War," *International Security*, vol. 15 (1990), pp. 5–54.
228. *International Herald Tribune*, May 12, 1992.
229. See Link, "Europäische Interessen an der Funktion der USA als europäische Balancemacht."
230. See Thomas Kielinger, "Nach der Revolution 1989/90: Die deutschen Interessen," in Mahncke, *Amerikaner in Deutschland*, p. 117.
231. On this alternative see Waltz, "The Emerging Structure of International Politics," pp. 71 ff.
232. See Ronald D. Asmus, Richard L. Kugler, and F. Stephen Larrabee, "It's Time for a New U.S.-European Strategic Bargain," *International Herald Tribune*, August 28/29, 1993.
233. See Schweigler, "The 'Go-Go Scenario,'" which also documents and analyzes the diverging American opinions.
234. Jacques Chirac, speech to the Académie des Sciences Morales et Politiques, June 17, 1991, *Le Monde*, June 19, 1991.
235. Jacques Amalric, "La France suggère à ses partenaires d'étudier une (doctrine) nucléaire pour l'Europe," *Le Monde*, February 12–13, 1992, cited in Lutz Schrader, "Mitterrands Europapolitik oder der lange Abschied vom Gaullismus," *Aus Politik und Zeitgeschichte*, vol. 43 (1993), p. 35.
236. See Schrader, "Mitterrands Europapolitik." After the present study had been completed it became known that, for the first time since France withdrew from NATO military structures in 1966, it would be taking part in a meeting of NATO defense ministers at the end of September 1994. See *Frankfurter Allgemeine Zeitung*, September 3, 1994.
237. Jean-Marie Guéhenno, "Sicherheit und Verteidigung in Europa," *Dokumente* (1992), pp. 121–27.
238. For a critical assessment of its effectiveness see Philip H. Gordon, *Die Deutsch-Französische Partnerschaft und die Atlantische Allianz* (Bonn: Europa Union Verlag, 1994).

239. This aspect was emphasized both in President Clinton's report, *A National Security Strategy of Engagement and Enlargement*, p. 34, and in the testimony of Assistant Secretary for European and Canadian Affairs Richard C. Holbrooke to the Foreign Affairs Committee of the U.S. Senate on August 10, 1994. See *Amerika Dienst*, August 17, 1994.
240. E. O. Czempiel comes to similar conclusions, even though his political science approach is a different one. See E. O. Czempiel. "Die Modernisierung der Atlantischen Gemeinschaft," *EA* (1990), pp. 275–86; and *Czempiel, Weltpolitik im Umbruch*, 2nd rev. ed. (Munich: Beck Verlag, 1993), pp. 40 ff.
241. On the incorporation of transatlantic relations into the framework of the CSCE see Bernard von Plate, ed., *Europa auf dem Wege zur kollektiven Sicherheit*? (Baden-Baden: Nomos Verlag, 1994), esp. Uwe Nerlich, "Das Zusammenwirken multinationaler institutionen," pp. 283–303.

Index

About the Authors

Miles Kahler is a senior fellow for international political economy at the Council on Foreign Relations and a professor of international relations at the Graduate School of International Relations and Pacific Studies, University of California, San Diego. His recent publications include *Regionalism and Rivalry: Japan and the U.S. in Pacific Asia* (co-editor with Jeffrey Frankel, 1993), *International Institutions and the Political Economy of Integration* (1995), and *Regional Futures and Transatlantic Economic Relations* (1995). Professor Kahler is chair of the editorial board of *International Organization* and a member of the editorial board of *World Politics*. He has been chair of the Committee on Foreign Policy Studies of the Social Science Research Council and currently serves as a member of the Executive Committee of the Program for International Studies in Asia.

Werner Link is a professor of political science at the University of Cologne. Previously he was a professor at the University of Marburg in 1971, at the University of Kassel from 1971 to 1975, and at the University of Trier from 1976 to 1990. Since 1992 Link has been chairman of the Federal Institute for Russian, East-European, and International Studies in Cologne. His publications include: *Die amerikanische Stabilisierungspolitik in Deutschland, 1921–32* (1970); *Das Konzept der friedlichen Kooperation und der Beginn des Kalten Krieges* (1971); *Der Ost-West-Konflikt. Die Organisation der internationalen Beziehungen im 20. Jahrhundert* (1980; including an English edition, *The East-West Conflict*, 1980); *Republik im Wandel. Die Ära Brandt, 1969–74* (co-authored with Karl Dietrich Bracher and Wolfgang Jäger, 1986); and *Republik im Wandel. Die Ära Schmidt, 1974–82* (co-authored with Wolfgang Jäger, 1987).

The Project on the Future of the Transatlantic Relationship

The project represents a comprehensive research initiative on the future of the relationship between Europe and the United States. The demise of the East-West conflict raises questions about the durability of the transatlantic partnership. The security bonds across the Atlantic are becoming brittle. The relationship is beginning to show signs of strain and destabilization. The post–Cold War era calls for a new kind of active and creative cooperation across the Atlantic. Americans and Europeans must base their partnership on a new, positive definition.

Against this background, the Bertelsmann Foundation decided to carry out a research project on the future of the transatlantic relationship in concert with the Research Group on European Affairs at the University of Munich and the Council on Foreign Relations in New York. The project aims to produce policy-oriented proposals for shaping the future relationship between the United States and Europe, thus contributing to three crucial objectives: redirecting transatlantic cooperation toward the realities and requirements of the new international situation, stimulating economic and social innovation on both sides, and promoting international stability.

At the center of the project is an interdisciplinary Strategy Group of about 30 members, made up of established experts from both sides of the Atlantic. The project also engages a new generation of leading intellectuals in the form of Working Groups. Both the Strategy Group and the Working Groups meet on a regular basis, alternating between locations in Europe and America. Discussions are conducted on the basis of studies and shorter papers prepared by group members, their associate institutions and outside experts. These analytical efforts result in concrete policy proposals that are circulated in the policy community. The project is also producing a book series, of which this volume is a part, to be published in both the United States and Europe.

The Project Partners

The Bertelsmann Foundation is committed to promoting innovation, generating ideas, injecting important issues into a broadly based debate, and, above all, helping to bring pressing problems closer to a solution. To accompany the process of political decision-making, the Bertelsmann Foundation, the Research Group on European Affairs at Munich University, and the Council on Foreign Relations launched in 1993 a project on "The Future of the Transatlantic Relationship." The goal of this project is to offer practical solutions to urgent political problems and to participate in formulating long-term strategies.

The Research Group on European Affairs is part of the Geschwister-Scholl-Institute for Political Science at the Ludwig-Maximilians-University in Munich. The Research Group is now integrated into the new Center for Applied Policy Research—CAP—and can look back on more than ten years of intensive research into European issues. The Research Group possesses comprehensive research and publication faciliities. These include editorial teams, a research library, and the European Documentation Center, which has all the documents issued by the European Community institutions on file. It also has access to the European database network. The Research Group organizes various ongoing research projects, publications series, conferences, and symposiums.

The Council on Foreign Relations is a nonprofit and nonpartisan membership organization dedicated to improving the understanding of U.S. foreign policy through the exchange of ideas. The Council's principal activities, conducted in New York City, Washington, D.C., and elsewhere in the United States and abroad, are coordinated by its Meeting Program, Studies Program, Corporate Program, and various national outreach programs for members and the general public. Since 1922, the Council has published *Foreign Affairs*, the preeminent journal in the field. The Council on Foreign Relations Press publishes books and occasional policy reports on a broad range of issues, which are made available to the public. The Council also produces "America and the World," a weekly radio series aired on National Public Radio and sponsors occasional televised policy hearings.